Exterminator

Exterminator

by E V A J O L E N E B O Y D

THOROUGHBRED
Legends®
No. 18

ECLIPSE
PRESS

Lexington, Kentucky

Library of Congress Control Number: 2002101618

ISBN 1-58150-087-4

Printed in The United States
First Edition: October 2002

Distributed to the trade by
National Book Network
4720-A Boston Way
Lanham, MD 20706
1.800.462.6420

a division of
The Blood-Horse, Inc.
PUBLISHERS SINCE 1916

EXTERMINATOR

CONTENTS

EXTERMINATOR

CHAPTER 1

"Why not Exterminator?"

Western Europe was at war in 1915, the year Exterminator was foaled. His arrival occurred as American racing struggled to regain its prominence after an enforced hiatus. Anti-gambling forces had begun shutting down many racetracks in 1908, though tracks in Kentucky and Maryland never closed and New York managed to stay open until 1911. By 1913 most tracks had reopened, but during the interim many owners had taken their stables to France and England.

On May 30, 1915, two years to the day after Belmont Park reopened, Fair Empress foaled the big chestnut colt by McGee at Almahurst Farm. Located near Nicholasville, Kentucky, twelve miles south of Lexington, Almahurst had been in the Knight family for some 150 years. The Knights had received the property as a land grant in the early nineteenth century, and ensuing generations became renowned as breeders of Thoroughbreds and Standardbreds.

Fair Empress came from great stock. She was bred by W.S. Barnes at his Melbourne Stud near Lexington. Her sire, Jim Gore, was a stakes-winning son of mighty Hindoo, one of the all-time great distance runners and winner of the 1881 Kentucky Derby. Appearing three times in Fair Empress' pedigree was the immortal sire Lexington, helping make the mare's lineage "...one of the stoutest families in the world." [1]

Fair Empress raced in the colors of P.H. McCarren and was unplaced in her only two starts, both at age two. Afterward she was returned to Melbourne Stud for the 1902 breeding season. She proved to be a sturdy producer. From 1903 through 1921, Fair Empress produced seventeen foals. Exterminator, the source of her place in Thoroughbred history, was twelfth.

The mating that produced Exterminator has about as many versions as Mrs. M.J. Mizner had sons, of which there seems to be at least four. W.P. Knight, who acquired Fair Empress a few years before Exterminator's foaling, was one. He was presumably the eldest, and when he died, date unknown, Almahurst passed into his mother's ownership. Some credit another son, G.L. Knight, a Nicholasville banker, with planning the union.

But according to an article in *The Thoroughbred Record*, Joseph Knight "made arrangements [in the spring of 1914] to breed three of his mother's mares to McGee," a fourteen-year-old stallion owned by Charles W. Moore of Mere Hill Stud. Moore was to have the pick of the mares owned by Mr. Knight's mother, and Fair Empress was among them. Moore thus retained shares in their get.

It is the fourth Mizner son, F.D. "Dixie" Knight, whose name appears as Exterminator's breeder of record. He's known to have handled the physical aspect and paperwork for breeding, foal registrations, and leasing stallions.

Bred by Lord Bradford in England and foaled in 1900, McGee was the only issue sired by White Knight before that stallion was gelded. Ed Corrigan, owner of Hawthorne Race Course near Chicago, purchased the yearling for "giveaway prices," and named him for his personal secretary, Tom McGee. In the United States the chestnut colt won twenty-four races.

In 1909 financial difficulties forced Corrigan to sell Hawthorne and his stable, ninety-two head that brought

only $22,995 altogether. Moore purchased McGee for $1,300. The stallion stood at Mere Hill, a farm two miles north of Lexington on Newtown Pike, until his death on September 18, 1931. McGee was successful in the breeding shed, leading the sire list for progeny earnings in 1922 with $222,491 and ranked in the top twenty in progeny earnings eleven times through 1940. Although McGee won at nine furlongs, he was more at home at shorter distances, yet he sired at least three true stayers in Exterminator, Firebrand, and In Memoriam and was the sire of Donerail, winner of the 1913 Kentucky Derby.

Exterminator was born into an age when horses were cast in such heroic molds that they remain legends a century later: Colin, Sysonby, Sir Barton, Man o' War. J.K.M. Ross, son of the prominent Canadian horseman, J.K.L. Ross, chronicled this era in his book *Boots and Saddles* and referred to this period as the Golden Age, of which he wrote, "Never has there been a period when the caliber of horses was as high and the racing as consistently keen." Due to fewer tracks and horses than now, Ross said the "battleground was narrower, and the giants repeatedly fought it out among themselves."

Ross also emphasized the human equation of the

Golden Age. "Illustrious horses called for men of comparable stature." The Belmonts, the Whitneys, and the Keenes, to name a few. And then, there was Willis Sharpe Kilmer, as colorful and illustrious as any other owner of the century and more than matching the extravagant times of the Golden Age.

In the world of high society, Willis Kilmer belonged to the nouveau riche and was not fully accepted as one of the established scions. During an Atlantic crossing aboard an ocean liner, Kilmer was snubbed by his more elite fellow passengers. "Here they were," Binghamton, New York, historian Floyd West wrote, "turning up their noses at a man who makes 35 to 50,000 dollars every day whether he gets out of bed or not." [2]

Kilmer gained his wealth — ill-gained by some accounts — from a medical concoction called Swamp Root (a.k.a. Swamproot).

Born in Brooklyn in 1868, Kilmer was ten when his father Jonas Kilmer moved the family to Binghamton, located at the confluence of the Chenango and Susquehanna rivers in western New York, where Jonas' brother, Dr. S. Andral Kilmer, had set up his medical practice in 1873. Dr. Kilmer was also a proficient chemist

and fashioned his own medicines from herbs. Using his sister's kitchen as his lab, Andral developed Swamp Root, said to cure whatever ails you, but more specifically kidney and liver diseases. The elixir, as well as his other medicines, advertised as "Standard Herbal Remedies," became so popular that Andral asked Jonas to leave New York City and move to Binghamton so Jonas could manage the business. With the company's subsequent success, they moved the lab and factory to a large brick building on the corner of Chenango and Virgil streets.

Willis Kilmer was attending Cornell University when he was asked to work for the business. The pharmacy was in admirable condition but wasn't growing like it should. Willis quickly identified the problem — lack of a wider market — and saw a potential goldmine. He dropped out of Cornell and took over the advertising, concentrating on the "Remedies" bestseller, Swamp Root. [3]

Willis Kilmer began saturating East Coast newspapers with ads. Then the campaign spread west. Even though the potion was never proven to have any real medicinal value — save for feelings of well-being

11

brought on by its nine percent alcohol content — Willis began including in the ads "letters from Swamp Root users" who swore to its effectiveness. Most of those letters had been written by Kilmer himself.

The company teetered on bankruptcy for a while, but the Kilmer fortunes finally turned around, Willis' fortunes in particular. His expertise in mass advertising attracted the attention of Joseph Pulitzer, owner of the *New York World*, who offered him $25,000 per year to manage the advertising department of his newspapers. Kilmer respectfully declined, saying, "If I am worth $25,000 a year to you, I am worth more than that to myself."

There were those who said he usurped his uncle's and father's business and wound up with the patent for Swamp Root through somewhat unethical means. But Jonas, prior to his death in 1912, said, "It was my son who made the Kilmer business big and successful." By 1903 Kilmer and Company was grossing more than two million dollars a year. [4]

Not everyone was impressed. When Binghamton's sole newspaper, the *Evening Herald*, attacked his motives, Kilmer countered by starting his own, the *Binghamton Press*, and built a twelve-story building in

1904 to house it. It was Binghamton's tallest building, and Kilmer is said to have made sure floors could be added in case someone built one taller.

Kilmer, who was obviously irritated by the negative criticism, admitted Swamp Root likely made him the "most unpopular man in the country." But he also sported a good sense of humor. When someone once asked him what the stuff was good for, Kilmer replied, "Oh, about three million dollars a year." Milton Bray, Exterminator's groom during the time Exterminator resided at Remlik Hall in Virginia, found another use for Swamp Root. Mixed with brown sugar, oats, grain, and olive oil, it made an excellent winter feed for the horses.

Kilmer delighted in everything that came with wealth. He enjoyed fast cars and drove one called the Green Demon in the Vanderbilt Cup. He loved luxurious cars, too, and imported a very pricey French Panhard; its accessories included a French chauffeur. He introduced golf to the Binghamton area and appeared on the links in flaming red cap and cloak. He owned two steam-driven yachts christened *Remlik* (Kilmer spelled backward), both of which Kilmer tendered to the government after the United States entered World War I in 1917. He owned

Sky Lake, a lodge in the mountains near Binghamton, and maintained a year-round suite at the Vanderbilt Hotel in New York.

But horses were a passion he inherited from his father. He often drove Jonas' Standardbreds in competition while his own jumpers racked up successes in Madison Square Garden. In 1909 he purchased some land in Middlesex County, Virginia, not far from where the Rappahannock River enters Chesapeake Bay, and began renovating a rambling fifty-two-room antebellum mansion that he named Remlik Hall.

His love of horses and compulsion for speed inevitably turned his attention to the Sport of Kings. In a December 1915 issue of *The Thoroughbred Record*, Kilmer was identified as a new recruit and had built yet another facility, a stud farm on Riverside Drive in Binghamton "that promises to become famous." At the time he had a string of "high-class yearlings in training under the direction of Frank M. Taylor." In 1916 Election became the first horse to carry Kilmer's green-and-orange silks with a brown sash to victory. In August of that year, Kilmer's future in racing turned dramatically.

The Saratoga yearling sales were still in their infan-

cy in 1916, but one local writer for *The Saratogian* predicted the event was more than a passing phenomenon. "Horsemen are of the opinion that Saratoga is gradually becoming the center for yearling sales," he wrote. "The fact that August is about the 'psychological moment,' when owners begin to think of buying yearlings, coupled with the circumstance that all of the big-moneyed owners are at Saratoga, have a good deal to do with the selection of this resort as the locale of so many sales." That year the sales were not held at night or on Sundays as they are now; instead, the sales were conducted in the racetrack paddock prior to the day's card.

Kilmer came to the sales primed to spend whatever it took to race and breed classic winners. His fledgling stable had a few runners at Saratoga, most of which were of the ilk of Election, who finished out of the money in the United States Hotel Stakes there.

Early in the meeting, Kilmer met forty-nine-year-old trainer Henry McDaniel, "Uncle Henry" to his many friends. McDaniel's name and reputation were well known to horsemen. It isn't clear if he was without a stable at the time; but at any rate, he was glad to

offer advice to this graying, forty-eight-year-old New
Yorker who exhibited an energy and intensity the sport
sorely needed. McDaniel was often seen in Willis' company, attending the races and examining yearlings in
the barns. It was one of those trips to the barns that
changed Willis Sharpe Kilmer's life.

Imported blood has always played a role in American
racing and breeding. In 1916 there was a much larger
than usual influx of youngsters from war-torn England
and France, exported, possibly, to save their lives. On
August 12, Kilmer purchased a yearling daughter of
Rock Sand from Clarence Mackay's Haras de Fresnay,
France, consignment. The $9,500 filly would stand as the
top-priced yearling that year. Later in the month, he
bought the racing age Tom McTaggart for $12,500 and
went as high as $17,000 for the three-year-old stakes
winner Dodge, but was outbid by one A. Kingsley
Macomber, one of the other "new" faces at Saratoga that
year. As the vagaries of the sport would have it, the filly
never got to the races. But one gamble did pay off.

Kilmer had already homed in on one of the two
dozen French yearlings from the Delbert Reiff consignment advertised for August 15. Most sources suggest it

was McDaniel who recommended Kilmer make a go at the colt that had piqued his interest. "He has some ringbones on his fores," McDaniel warned, "but they're high. I don't think they'll hinder him." The colt was a striking bay son of Sundridge—Sweet Briar II, by St. Frusquin, and bred by Comte Castelbajac. In the French tradition, the yearling was already named — Sunday. Kilmer was instantly smitten with the colt and visited his stall on numerous occasions, leaving a hefty twenty-dollar tip with the colt's handler each time.

Although many buyers were turned off by the ringbones (a bony growth at the top of the hoof or near the pastern), the bidding was lively. The colt ultimately went to Kilmer for six-thousand dollars, the second highest-priced yearling at the 1916 sales and thus giving Kilmer the distinction of having purchased both the top-priced filly and colt, whom he renamed Sun Briar, that year.

Meanwhile, other youngsters changed hands without the news and the big bucks, the average that year being $932. Among this "silent" majority were some yearlings quietly purchased by Lexington owner/trainer J. Cal Milam from the Powers-Hunter Company's paddock sale. Milam bought a bay son of Fitzherbert for $1,150 on August 12 and a week later came away with four colts, including two sons of McGee. One cost him six hundred dollars. The other, a tall and rangy chestnut colt from the F.D. Knight/Charles Moore consignment went for $1,500. Most prospective buyers ignored him as too lean and "growthy." But Milam fancied him straight off. "...he was right good looking," he said years later, "and he was well bred and I got him at what I considered a cheap price." [5]

There's no record of whether Willis Kilmer ever saw him. But in one of those sequences of seemingly divergent events that make history, Kilmer's acquisition of the royally bred Sunday would actually lead to crossing paths with the son of McGee.

As for the sales themselves, they boded well for the future, said *The New York Times*:

"No better evidence of the healthy condition of racing was given at Saratoga than by the wonderful prices paid for yearlings...Including the foreign importations, nearly 200 horses have been bought in the last six weeks by either newcomers to the turf or by owners who have felt the necessity of increasing their stables by the infusion of new and young blood."

Returning to Lexington, Milam sent his yearlings to the Kentucky Association track for breaking and early schooling. The first time he saw the McGee—Fair Empress colt under tack, Milam thought he had something. Later, he asked his wife to suggest a name for a runner he boldly predicted would vanquish his opponents.

Mrs. Milam laughed. "Why not Exterminator?"

So, *American Stud Book* number 84,588 now had a name.

CHAPTER 2

"a wild 'un in the nursery"

J. Calvin Milam didn't see his first racehorses until he was nineteen years old.

Born July 17, 1872, in Sheffield, Alabama, Milam first planned on being a physician. That is until the spring of 1892 when he visited a cousin in Lexington who took him for an afternoon of racing at the Kentucky Association track. He went home, packed a bag, told his parents he was going into the horse business, and returned to Lexington.

Milam soon learned that the horse business can be a rough furrow to plow. He worked on John Turner's farm near Paris "...one whole winter without pay, just for the experience." [1]

The following spring he took odd jobs around the barns and finally saved enough to buy two cheap racers, Hilyar and Miss Rosa. He won some races with them and bought a few more horses. With his finances stretched a bit thin, Milam went to work training "Pa" Bradley's horses over the winter of 1896-1897 and did so well that J.S. Wadsworth hired him that summer to handle his small string. Again, Milam revealed his Midas touch when it came to horses, and Wadsworth offered him a permanent job. The idea of a steady paycheck was tempting, but Milam decided to devote all his efforts toward developing his own stable. Later, Milam attributed much of his success to John E. Madden, owner of Hamburg Place and one of the most prolific breeders of outstanding gallopers in the late-nineteenth and early-twentieth centuries. Madden is said to have tutored the young trainer and whenever a particular strategy turned into success, Milam would say, "…learned it from John Madden. Smartest horseman I ever knew."

Cal Milam found it was more worthwhile to buy promising yearlings, race them one, maybe two years, and then turn them over for a profit. This was called a "sales stable," and Milam did so well with that method that it wasn't long before he was able to purchase 531 acres on Tates Creek Pike near Lexington. He named

the farm Merrick Place, after a gelding he always said
was the best horse he had ever raced.

Merrick was his first big horse. Milam bought him
as a chronically lame three-year-old in 1906 and
nursed him to health. Merrick raced the remainder of
his career under Milam's green-and-gold colors
(Milam did lose Merrick in a claiming race in New
Orleans but claimed him back the next race) and
retired in 1915 having won sixty-one of his 205 starts.
In advanced age, Merrick went blind and lost his
teeth, necessitating a special diet. But Milam continued to care for him and Merrick lived to be thirty-
eight years old, putting him in the *Guinness Book of
World Records* as the oldest Thoroughbred on record. [2]
Such honesty and devotion spoke highly of Cal
Milam, a man described as one of the "kindliest" of
Kentucky's "older generation of horsemen."
Incredibly, Milam never had a losing season. Horses
just seemed to want to do their best for him.

Milam was forty-five in 1917 when he moved his
two-year-olds from the farm to the track in Lexington
as he did each February and March. Now their serious
training began and Milam hoped to have them ready

for Lexington's spring meeting. It soon became evident that Exterminator wouldn't be.

The colt hadn't been the most generous-looking yearling, too rangy. But Milam thought he would fill out over the winter. Instead, the horse's weight gain didn't keep pace with his growth. Now he was a sorry-looking individual, and Milam had him castrated. "In the spring of 1917," wrote Kent Hollingsworth in *The Great Ones*, "Exterminator became so poor and run-down that Milam decided he would have to castrate the colt." But not everyone agreed as to the reason behind the neutering. Lew Koch wrote that Exterminator was gelded because of "a wild disposition..."

Bob Considine, racing columnist for the *Daily Mirror*, was more specific. "We picked it up piece-meal from Cal Milam...," he wrote in 1942. "Exterminator, who was to set records for patience, was a wild 'un in the nursery of his breeder, F.D. Knight, and even wilder when Milam bought him for $1,500 early in his life. Milam had him gelded for his own sake..." As incredible as it seems in light of the Exterminator we know, no less than Colonel Matt Winn, the man whose guidance made the Kentucky Derby what it is today, verified that when Milam "found that he had a colt with a fretful nature, and a wild disposition. He had the colt gelded, which gentled him."

Racing historian John Hervey, however, who wrote under the sobriquet "Salvator," argued that Exterminator wasn't gelded because of health or temperament, but simply because he wasn't fashionably bred. "We must remember, that when he was begotten, his sire, McGee, did not enjoy his present high estate as a progenitor." [3]

Hervey failed to mention that McGee had already sired a Kentucky Derby winner, Donerail. Adding to his opinion on McGee's background, he said, "In short, he was merely a selling plater of something above ordinary class...he was not even 'thoroughbred.' He came — or comes — from one of those native, non-figure families whence we have been so persistently taught, nothing good can be expected. That is, nothing fit to be a sire..."

As for Exterminator, he was gelded before "he was of an age to do any mischief in the world...All there was left for him to do was to go out and race. And, in the words of the prophet, he has 'gone and done it.' " [4]

Exterminator didn't debut until June 30 at the

northern Kentucky track Latonia, now Turfway. One of two non-starters in the field of a dozen maidens, he was the second choice at 5.20-1 mainly off his recent strong workouts. John Morys, the first of eighteen jockeys who would ride Exterminator during his career, allowed him to cover four furlongs in :48 3/5, then restrained him over the last quarter to win by three lengths, getting the six furlongs in 1:14 4/5.

Two weeks later Exterminator faced ten rivals in a five-furlong allowance race at Windsor in Ontario and finished fourth. It was a good effort, considering he'd been knocked about late in the race and closed from seventh in the last furlong. Three days later heavy rains at Windsor gave the gelding his first opportunity to handle an off track, and he won by a length.

July 26 found him at Kenilworth Park in Ontario and in the role of favorite, for the first time, in an allowance at five and a half furlongs. The race ended in a four-horse blanket finish, with Exterminator the last under the wire but only a half-length out of first. He came out of the race with a muscle strain, and Milam shelved him for the rest of the year.

It had been a decent season, and Milam was pleased

with him. He customarily nominated all his yearlings to the Kentucky Derby, a selling point he had learned under Madden, and was particularly glad he had done so with this one. Soon enough the Derby would play a big role in Exterminator's future.

Willis Sharpe Kilmer had been totally galvanized by the Saratoga scene: the energy that rippled through the barns and sales paddocks; hyper yearlings, any one of which could be a Colin or Sysonby; the excitement and rivalry of the bidding; the idea that for little more than pocket change, he could buy a Sun Briar. The ebullience carried through late fall when he cabled his London agent instructing him to buy "the best yearling colt that he could obtain in England." [5]

After hiring Henry McDaniel at Saratoga in August 1916, Kilmer ordered him to go to England in time for the December sales at Newmarket, where he was to buy the best-bred mares he could find for Sun Briar's future court. This task was accomplished despite a little complication called war that made every voyage into English waters a gauntlet of German U-boats. Officially the United States was still neutral, but Germany had warned it couldn't guarantee U.S. citizens' safety. Even passenger liners were subject to attack, a point made all too clear in 1915 when a U-boat sent the *Lusitania* and some 1,400 civilians to the bottom.

McDaniel breathed a sigh of relief upon his return. He brought back several nice mares, including Contessina, the future dam of Reigh Count. But some of his purchases weren't so lucky. Several others, including the best of the lot, a mare named Brownie, had to take a later ship due to breeding commitments. Their vessel was tagged by a U-boat and sunk.

In the meantime, Kilmer had grown increasingly excited about the yearling purchase he had renamed Sun Briar. The colt was a handsome individual, a compact bay with a star and a snip his only markings. He had a robust build, with a deep neck set on powerful shoulders, indicating more of a sprinting propensity. While Kilmer's $9,500 filly, whom he named Conference, never reached the races, Sun Briar went on to a juvenile championship.

Under Arthur Pickens, Sun Briar lost his first two starts, a maiden and an allowance. But he turned heads in his next outing, the Great American Stakes at Aqueduct, with William Knapp aboard. After stumbling badly, he came back to edge stakes winner Lucullite, from whom he was getting sixteen pounds. Trailing the field was the pro tem division leader, Papp, whose odd name derived from his owner G.W. Loft's candy-making slogan, "Penny a Pound Profit."

Sun Briar and Papp met again and Papp beat him in both the Whirl Stakes at Empire City and the United States Hotel Stakes at Saratoga. Then Sun Briar turned his season around and dominated the remainder of the Spa's meeting, winning the Albany Handicap; the Saratoga Special from Papp, under equal weights of 122 pounds; the Grand Union Hotel Stakes, with 130 pounds; and in his last start of the year, the Hopeful Stakes and its rich $30,600 purse. He carried equal weight of 130 pounds with Papp in that race. There were no official championships then, but Sun Briar was conceded the championship for his age group off of his five wins (all stakes), a second, and two thirds in nine outings.

His earnings total of $58,505 not only topped his own division, but was the most amassed by any other horse that year, including Kentucky Derby winner Omar Khayyam and the handicap champion Old Rosebud. The amount made up most of Kilmer's racing

revenues, which in the race for the year's top money-winning owner, placed him second by less than four thousand to A.K. Macomber's $68,578.

Kilmer himself was becoming accepted by the circle of the "old-money" millionaires such as the Vanderbilts and the Wideners. His presence was commanding, standing in winner's circles in straw hat and holding a cane. "He was a good-looking man of impressive proportions with a voice in keeping with his size," J.K.M. Ross wrote. "He was generous in the extreme, a great philanthropist...a gentleman of somewhat eccentric habits."

Ross' phrase, "...of somewhat eccentric habits," could be an understatement. Take the famous dinner parties Kilmer hosted at Remlik Hall, his training farm in Virginia, as described by Ross:

"...there were several houses on his large estate and when he was entertaining at dinner in one house, he would suddenly announce in the middle of a meal that the remaining courses would be served in one of the other houses. The move would be made with varying degrees of enthusiasm from his guests and I often wondered with what reaction from his chef."

Ross liked Kilmer, though, and thought him to be

"an open-hearted and kindly soul who loved racing in the true sense of the word. And his deep affection for his horses was nothing less than inspiring."

Some, however, saw Kilmer's obsession for Sun Briar run to the extreme, like the horse's "welcome home parade." While Exterminator retired quietly for the winter to Merrick Place, Sun Briar came home to a brass band and good wishes from a big percentage of Binghamton's 1917 population of 60,000. The *Binghamton Press* recorded the event:

"Ten thousand persons crowded the railroad station here yesterday to greet Sun Briar, W.S. Kilmer's great two-year-old, after his successful season at Saratoga. A unique parade which followed was the signal for a city wide celebration, arranged by the Chamber of Commerce.

"The procession was headed by the Municipal band, after which came a detachment of the 1st Ambulance Company. More than 150 equestrians followed, with Sun Briar and Willis Sharpe Kilmer, the owner, bringing up the rear. Jockey Willie Knapp was decorated with a great horseshoe of flowers."

On January 1, the universal birthday for all

Thoroughbreds, Kilmer threw the biggest birthday party Binghamton had ever seen, at least for a horse. The gala was held at Kilmer's new showplace in Binghamton, Sun Briar Court, and attracted "hundreds of horse lovers...to pay tribute to the world's greatest thoroughbred colt, the great son of Sundridge and Sweet Briar...," the *Binghamton Press* reported.

Sun Briar Court spread over some five hundred acres. Charles Herring, who visited in 1922, described it as an estate "situated within the city limits [of Binghamton] and surrounded by beautiful homes, on both sides of the historic and enchantingly beautiful Susquehanna River..." Visitors toured the clubhouse where artifacts from the colt's campaign were displayed, including the one thousand dollar plate won in the Saratoga Special and the shoes Sun Briar wore winning the rich Hopeful Stakes. The clubhouse also contained an "extensive gallery of equine pictures, some of them exceedingly rare, [and] is alone worth a long journey to see." [6]

One would be safe in referring to Sun Briar's birthday party as the social event of the year.

"From 2 o'clock until 6, lower Riverside Drive was

alive with motors filled with merry parties, eager to see the champion two-year-old, to inspect the new track, opened yesterday for the first time; to visit the Club House with its mementos of Sun Briar's triumphs, and to enjoy Mr. Kilmer's cordial hospitality. Hundreds of others braved the keen air and walked from the car line, and they found themselves amply repaid for the effort by the afternoon's pleasures.

"The visitors yesterday hurried to Sun Briar's stable, where the champion held court. Then each of the other thoroughbreds was visited and each received his meed of admiration.

"A tramp around the big, covered, electrically-lighted exercising ring gave the visitors an idea of the completeness of the plant, which has been provided so that the horses may be kept constantly fit. Back of the exercising ring, they found the broodmare stables...where the expectant dams are housed. Complete as the plan is, Mr. Kilmer has prepared plans to replace the present stables after the war with stables of steel and tile construction throughout..." [7]

Three tracks completed the place: an indoor quarter-mile oval; another that Herring described as a "superb

straightaway along the river" and still another that was modeled after England's Sandown course. The resident stallions included the three-year-old Sun Briar (who would cover some mares early the next spring) and the English-breds Assagai and Allumeur. There were also thirty-eight mares in residence, including Sun Briar's dam, Sweet Briar II; Conference; Contessina; and Hussy, Kilmer's first winning filly.

So in two worlds much farther apart than the miles that separated Binghamton and Lexington, Sun Briar would emerge as the most anticipated three-year-old in years, while Exterminator was merely one name among seventy nominated to the 1918 Kentucky Derby.

His anonymity would soon be coming to an end.

EXTERMINATOR

CHAPTER 3

"The most disappointed man in Kentucky"

Louisville is home of horse racing's premier event, the Kentucky Derby, but Lexington, some eighty miles east, is the cradle of racing in Kentucky. Founded in 1779, Lexington was settled mostly by Virginians. A good many of them were horsemen who brought with them their Virginia blue bloods. Scarcely had the first streets been laid out than the male gentry were matching their steeds against each other. There's mention of racing on the "Commons," present Water Street, about 1787, but a marker on South Broadway indicates the cradle of Kentucky racing:

FIRST RACE COURSE
Near this spot, pioneers in 1780 established the starting point of the first race path in Kentucky extending southward one quarter of a mile.

Street racing had its obvious setbacks. "Must our lives and limbs be placed in danger or lose a day's or week's chores in the village while the men indulge in their folly?" the women of Lexington complained. So, racing was banned and horsemen looked elsewhere, finally settling on Lee's Woods, a little west of town, now the site of the Lexington Cemetery. They built Williams Race Track, "a very eccentric oval, with sharp turns." [1]

Racing eventually outgrew the small course, and on July 29, 1826, sixty of Kentucky's most prominent horsemen met at Mrs. Sanford Keen's Tavern — the site of the Phoenix Hotel — and founded the Kentucky Association for the Improvement of the Breeds of Stock. Two years later, the Kentucky Association track, often just called Lexington, or simply the K.A. — the initials inscribed on the winning post — was built at present Race and East Fifth streets. It held its inaugural meet that October, 1828. Where a federal housing project now stands, such cracks as Lexington, Ten Broeck, and Aristides raced, as did Sun Briar and Exterminator; Man o' War bid his fans farewell there in 1920. The K.A.'s days ended in 1934, replaced by the new Keeneland Race Course that opened west of town on Versailles Road. Part of the old track still lives, however; its winning post stands at Keeneland's entrance.

The Kentucky Association track was the oldest racing organization in America, according to Turf historian Walter S. Vosburgh, and hadn't failed to hold a meeting "with the possible exception of 1863, when 'wasteful war in all its fury burned...' "

In 1918 the track was ninety years old, and its continuity and traditions had made its spring meeting popular with horsemen, especially those prepping for the Kentucky Derby in Louisville.

In mid-February Cal Milam moved his horses from Merrick Place across town to the Kentucky Association track. He anticipated good things from several of his runners, including Exterminator, who had filled out some over the winter and was beginning to look like a solid racing machine. By April the gelding was stripped for hard work, and it wasn't long before he began turning heads.

Henry McDaniel shipped Sun Briar and his barn mates to Churchill Downs in mid-March. Kilmer's star

would train there for the Derby, although he was scheduled to make his three-year-old debut sometime during the Lexington meeting.

Everything indicated Sun Briar was training well as of early April, as evidenced by a "strong gallop" on the 8th, "...the crack colt speeding three furlongs in good time...and was preliminary to a try-out of a mile as soon as the track dries out thoroly [sic]." [2]

Certainly Sun Briar was the horse of the moment. As last year's juvenile champion, he was an over-whelmingly popular choice to win the Kentucky Derby. Winn's predictions that Sun Briar's presence would swell the Derby attendance to record proportions attest to the drawing power of his name. And Sun Briar certainly held pride of place in Kilmer's affections. The colt was his golden boy, perhaps even the validation of his place in the racing world. Quite possibly the gleam in Kilmer's eye when he spoke of him reflected his confidence in a Sun Briar Derby victory.

"No sucker horse is going to beat him," wrote Walter Pearce of the *Louisville Courier-Journal*, "even if they step four miles." Handicapper Emil Herz' annual Derby odds listed Sun Briar at 3 1/2-1. Exterminator's name was absent from the twenty-two named entries, but likely fell under the "other entrants" with odds ranging from 100-1 to 200-1.

Sun Briar looked to be on track for a Derby victory until April 14 when he bolted during a workout. "He was rank when he felt the whip," Knapp told McDaniel. But many believed the ringbones were bothering him. McDaniel assured the press the growths were "too high to prove seriously detrimental." [3]

As Sun Briar's media support began to erode, attention turned to possible successors, including T.C. McDowell's Plum, who recently had turned in the best mile at Lexington so far, 1:41 2/5; and Kenneth Alexander's Escoba, one of the previous year's top juveniles. Exterminator in the meantime had been working with a sprinting stablemate named Solly and had turned in some crackerjack times. On April 15 Exterminator stepped six furlongs in 1:15 flat, less than four seconds off the track record.

Sun Briar redeemed himself with a mile worked in 1:47 and a second on April 19 in 1:45, a "wonderful showing for a colt in early training," wrote Paul Purman in the *Lexington Leader*. McDaniel was delighted and

loaded him on an eastbound train to Lexington to make his long-anticipated first start of the year.

Exterminator continued to look more and more like a serious Derby contender. On Saturday, April 20, Exterminator was clocked a mile in 1:42 2/5. "This horse is Milam's own entry," I.N. Parrish reported in the *Leader*, "and is proving faster with each trial." By April 22, Exterminator's pre-Derby odds had dropped to 50-1.

Thus, forces were set in motion for an event that was, at the time, little more than a footnote in the newspapers but would later prove to be one of racing's milestones: W.S. Kilmer's purchase of Exterminator.

Lexington's race meeting opened on Tuesday, April 23. A heavy rain that night left the track on Wednesday morning coated with a "slippery, treacherous mud." Trainers with proven mud horses went ahead with their schedules. One was Escoba's trainer John S. Ward. The colt plowed four furlongs through the goo in :54 flat.

Since Sun Briar had shown he could handle an off track, McDaniel's plans to start him in a six-furlong purse on Thursday the 25th went ahead. On race day Willis and Esther Kilmer arrived in high style in his Pierce Arrow. He told McDaniel about all the friends from Binghamton he had invited to a Derby victory party next month in the winner's circle. Filled with confidence, he then settled down to watch his colt take up where the juvenile champion had left off last year.

The result was a shocker. "How the mighty have fallen!" wrote a first-year journalism student out of the University of Kentucky named Thomas Rust Underwood. "Sun Briar...has been splashed with the mud of a rank outsider..." [4] That rank outsider was 37-1 shot Jim Heffering, whose time for the six furlongs, 1:17 2/5, was more than six seconds slower than the track standard. Even 49-1 Choir Master beat Sun Briar for second. Knapp said Sun Briar sulked again. McDaniel knew only that the colt wouldn't be ready for ten furlongs in sixteen days.

Kilmer was crushed. "Promise me, Henry, that Sun Briar will win the Derby." To which McDaniel replied, "If I could guarantee the horse would win, I would take $1,000 and make a five-horse parlay. And then I would have more money than you have." [5]

Sun Briar galloped on Saturday the 27th. Later that day, Willis Kilmer met Cal Milam at the Phoenix Hotel and Exterminator changed hands.

"It is plain to be seen," wrote Lexington journalist C.J. Savage in the *Louisville Courier-Journal*, "that Mr. Kilmer is not satisfied with the showing of Sun Briar...and he is looking about for better representation in it. Exterminator has been working good here..."

The *Daily Racing Form* also reported the sale on April 28, leaving no doubt about the date. But the events prior to the sale are fuzzy. The traditional story says that McDaniel saw Exterminator work a mile in 1:40, but this writer found nothing to substantiate that time.

Just as frustrating has been determining the purchase price, an amount that varies from nine thousand dollars cash plus two yearling fillies worth five hundred dollars each, on up to fifteen thousand dollars. Most are in accord with the nine-thousand-dollar-plus figure. The next most popular amount, fifteen thousand, accounts for about twenty percent of the reported accounts. Years later McDaniel recalled, "It was ten thousand dollars, of which nine thousand dollars was in cash and the remainder in the form of two maiden fillies by Ogden, valued for purposes of the trade at five hundred dollars each."

Savage's article published in the *Courier-Journal* the day after the Derby tells how Milam "...invested

$10,000 of the $15,000 which he got for the horse in Liberty bonds, making the purchases at the booth on the grounds of the Kentucky Association track."

During a 1978 interview with *Binghamton Press* writer Jack Shay, Willis Kilmer's second wife, Mrs. E.H. Ellison, said that the "$9,000 price tag was a mere pittance to Kilmer...and the two horses in trade were inconsequential. 'My lord,' Mrs. Ellison remembers her husband saying. 'I wanted to get rid of those two mares anyway.' "

One more version of the events comes from John E. Madden, who apparently owned a share in Exterminator with Milam. Madden, who was visiting a neighbor, W. Rodes Estill, received a phone call. He talked briefly, hung up, and turned to Estill. "Just sold a gelding worth $4,000," he said with a chuckle. "Got $9,000 and two fillies for him." [6]

Nevertheless, the deal was done, and Exterminator became Sun Briar's stablemate.

Despite Sun Briar's erratic and less-than-stellar performance, Kilmer, perhaps, still held high hopes for a Sun Briar victory in the Derby. However, the pre-Derby workouts between the champion two-year-old and his recently purchased work horse served only to dispel those hopes and frustrate Kilmer.

The workouts between Exterminator and Sun Briar are another point of confusion. The first one occurred soon after the horses arrived in Louisville on Sunday, April 28.

"It was a sad day..." Horace Wade wrote in *The Thoroughbred Record*. "It was a short jog, and Sun Briar finished so far in front that he looked lonesome. Kilmer, an irascible and choleric character, flew into a rage. 'You've bought me nothing but a billy goat!' "

But at a longer distance a few days later, "it was Exterminator in front at the end. The workout merely pointed out one thing to Kilmer — that Sun Briar was not ready for the Derby."

But Henry McDaniel had a different perspective: "The very first time Sun Briar and Exterminator hooked up in a workout the latter made the imported colt 'like it,' as (Exterminator) was full of run all of the way, and according to those who witnessed the trial he would have beaten him at any stage of the journey." [7]

Matt Winn, Churchill Downs' vice president and general manager, witnessed all three pre-Derby workouts, including the one just after the stable's return from Lexington. "It was a short jog," wrote Winn, "and Sun Briar finished well in front of Exterminator, who didn't have getaway speed. Kilmer had a lot of sharp things to say to Henry for agreeing to pay $12,000 for a 'truck horse.' " But when Exterminator beat Sun Briar their next time out, Kilmer said the gelding wasn't faster, Sun Briar just wasn't fit.

On May 7 a large crowd of media and horsemen turned out in the light rain of early Tuesday morning to watch Sun Briar try and beat War Cloud's incredible trial of the day before in which he set a training record for ten furlongs of 2:05 1/5. Sun Briar, with Bill Knapp up, was accompanied by Exterminator and stablemate Nelsweep. After limbering up with a jog around the course and leaving Nelsweep at the half-mile point, Sun Briar broke with Exterminator at the head of the stretch.

Sun Briar reeled off the first furlong in :12 flat and the next in :11 4/5. Nelsweep joined him at the half, clocked in :48 2/5. The next quarter slowed to :26 2/5, and the mile was reached in 1:42. By now Sun Briar's smooth strides had become choppy and he labored to get the final quarter in :30 4/5. His final time for the ten furlongs, 2:12 4/5.

Winn also witnessed the work. "...McDaniel sent out Sun Briar for a final route sharpener, together with Exterminator...I saw the work, which was on a heavy track. Obviously, something was wrong with Sun Briar, and after the trial Kilmer declared Sun Briar out of the Derby — the most disappointed man in Kentucky."

Exterminator's role in the trial wasn't mentioned beyond the break; yet the inference now was that Kilmer had purchased the gelding for the Derby. Such talk infuriated Kilmer, who released this statement:

"In view of certain misleading press reports regarding my purchase of Exterminator, I desire to say that I did not acquire this horse as a Derby candidate, but...as a trial horse for Sun Briar...In fact at the time of purchase I did not know Exterminator was eligible for the Derby. Buying Exterminator was in accordance with instructions to my trainer issued months ago, and is a well established part of my plan in getting Sun Briar ready for the great classic...It is also equally well understood that I do not consider Exterminator in the same class with Sun Briar."

Kilmer's statement that he instructed McDaniel to buy a gelding months ago was in direct contradiction to Milam's recollection that McDaniel was convinced to buy Exterminator only after he learned the gelding was eligible for the Derby.

On Friday morning of Derby Eve, the owners had to commit $250 and drop their hopeful's name in the entry box. One name that wouldn't be dropped in was Sun Briar. But Kilmer, sorely disappointed that his star would not be running, had what he considered a second-string player on his bench. It was a matter of deciding whether to assuage his disappointment by entering Exterminator. At some point after Sun Briar's poor run on Wednesday, Kilmer sought advice from a neutral perspective, someone he respected. In Louisville that person was Matt Winn.

The credit Winn has been given of saving the Kentucky Derby is well founded. Unlike such older stakes as the Travers at Saratoga, the Derby boasted an unbroken continuity since its inception in 1875. But it nearly ended with the 1902 running. In October of that year, Churchill Downs' secretary, Charlie Price, placed an ultimatum before Matt Winn: he had to buy the track. "If you don't, the Derby dies."

Winn was thirteen when he stood on the seat of his father's grocery wagon parked in the infield and watched Aristides win the first Kentucky Derby. He had seen every one of them since. Winn wasn't a horseman; he owned a successful Louisville men's clothing store. He did play the horses on occasion, but never to excess. His family was his first priority. Now Charlie Price was talking forty thousand dollars for a facility that had yet to make a profit.

Winn thought back to the boy who did extra chores for his dad in "world's record time" so that he could go with him to the opening of the new track and see the big race that had been patterned after the "darby" in England. "It was a thrill for me." The thought of never seeing another one... "I'd say 'No' and make it stick for a thousand years," he told Charlie Price, "if it involved anything but the Derby. But they mustn't stop running that race."

Winn's narrative of the process that saved the Kentucky Derby is best appreciated in his autobiography, *Down the Stretch*. When other tracks closed during the blackout, Winn kept the Downs open, for the Derby, for the sport, and for horsemen like Willis Kilmer.

When a dejected Kilmer entered Winn's office, the congenial general manager was sitting behind his desk, his leather chair creaking with every move of his stout frame. He was fifty-six with thinning hair, and he was impeccably dressed in a vested suit. A cigar in one hand or the other seemed as much a part of his attire as the perfectly folded handkerchief in his coat pocket. He had kind eyes and an honest face. In later years, one was struck by his resemblance to Winston Churchill.

"Who was that horse you had working with Sun Briar?" Winn asked, to which Kilmer snapped, "A truck horse named Exterminator that Henry McDaniel got me hooked for $12,000."

"If the boy hadn't been checking him down when he tried to run past Sun Briar—"

Kilmer stood. "That horse isn't fast enough to run past me," he said and stormed out. When Kilmer had calmed down, he saw Winn again later. "If he were your horse, would you start him?" Winn said he would. "All right. He starts."

So the 1918 Kentucky Derby was set. "...all that remains," one writer predicted, "to make the afternoon

memorable in the track's long history is a good brand of weather."

It would take more than a good brand of weather to get Kilmer past his disappointment. It would take a lanky, long-legged miracle.

CHAPTER 4

"...king of the thoroughbred world"

Forty years after Matt Winn had watched the first Derby from his father's wagon, eight-year-old David Alexander perched on his father's shoulders so he could see the track and root Regret home on her history-making Derby victory. She had been his first bet, and she returned his two dollars plus $5.30 more.

Three years later Alexander had his heart set on a new "bike with carbide lamps and other stylish accessories." A War Cloud victory at 2-1 wouldn't do it. He needed longer odds. So he handed his father the two dollars he had saved doing odd jobs and asked him to put it on number five who was close to 30-1. Did he have a hunch on the number five horse in the fifth race? "My betting in those days was always intuitive," the Turf writer and historian wrote years later. "I had liked Exterminator, who didn't figure to have a chance, solely because a horse with such a name could not possibly lose."

A handful of others also liked the "five/five" combination, like the fellow in the betting pavilion — said to have the "tenacity born of red liquor" — shouting to anyone who would listen, "Remember, boys, two fives is lucky: it's Exterminator." [1]

Back in February, Winn had projected that this year's renewal would be "one of the greatest races in the history of the event...depending on how the horses trained." [2] Due to Sun Briar's popularity, Winn anticipated a record crowd, surpassing the previous year's 40,000.

But by the second Saturday in May — the Derby held on the first day of the meeting in those days — many of the big guns from 1917 hadn't made the cut. Not Papp, Sun Briar's runner-up as juvenile champion, or the iron-legged Tippity Witchet. Or Sun Briar himself. Still, Winn had no complaints about the ten names dropped into the entry box on Friday.

He was just grateful there was going to be a Derby this year.

It had been a year since the United States declared war

on Kaiser Wilhelm's Germany. "It'll be over in six months," many predicted. Instead, America suffered heavy losses with German U-boats using the waters off the East Coast as a shooting gallery. Some Americans believed it was no time to be going to racetracks or any other sporting venues.

Earlier that year, a Louisville journalist had called for the cancellation of the spring meeting and a suspension of all racing for the duration of the war. Troubled, Winn contacted Admiral Cary Grayson, President Woodrow Wilson's personal physician. Would he get the president's opinion on this? Grayson said he would. It wasn't long before the admiral notified Winn that President Wilson wanted racing to continue. Winn next met with American Red Cross representatives about what was needed and was told the organization was woefully short of funds.

"I then pledged them 10 per cent of all money handled at the Churchill Downs meeting. The employees gave 10 per cent of their salary; the track gave 10 per cent of its 'take.' And the horsemen gave 10 per cent of their earnings." Winn even planted the infield with potatoes, which were also in short supply. "We raised

about 1,000 bushels," he wrote in *Down the Stretch*. "They were auctioned off in barrel lots, the money to go to the Red Cross, and some of the barrels sold for as high as $100 each." Moreover, Churchill Downs and other tracks hosted War Savings Stamps and Liberty Bonds booths, and a war tax was added to the price of admission tickets.

Horsemen and fans came through again when it became known the military was short of field glasses. According to a Navy representative, four-fifths of all the field glasses donated nationwide came from the racing industry. So from a trench somewhere in France or from the deck of a warship, an American officer observed the enemy through a pair of glasses that a George Widener or Willis Kilmer may have used to watch the Kentucky Derby weeks earlier.

The Derby had survived another close call; now all that was needed was that "good brand of weather." But "Rain or shine," Walter Pearce wrote in the *Louisville Courier-Journal*, "great horses will face the barrier, and the greatest of all races of the American turf will attract many thousand spectators to the course even in a downpour."

Saturday dawned with the twin spires bathed in

bright sunshine. There was no hint of rain and everyone wondered if Old Rosebud's track and Derby record
of 2:03 3/5 would still be standing at day's end. The
good weather didn't last long. Clouds began rolling in
and by eight o'clock were spilling rain. Immediately,
Aurum and Jim Heffering were scratched. Over the
next five hours, 2.31 inches fell, still a record for Derby
Day, and by post time, the track was listed as muddy
for the race for only the second time.

The rain deepened Kilmer's gloom, and as he made
his way to his box, well-intentioned sympathies over
Sun Briar and offers of good luck for Exterminator
only made matters worse. It would be just his luck that
the gelding couldn't run a lick in the mud.

But something happened just as the afternoon's cer-
emonies began, so timely that a stage director couldn't
have cued it any better. Following the call to the post
for the first race, the band struck the first notes to the
national anthem as the color guard raised the flag. At
the moment the banner reached the top of the staff,
the sun broke through the clouds and the colors
snapped to attention in a sudden breeze. One writer
thought it very omen-like. "...a resplendent guaran-

tee," he wrote, "to the freedom of the nation...that our fighting forces and their allies will make the world safe for democracy."

With the sun, the mood of the crowd perked up, and throughout the undercard, conversation centered around Sun Briar's absence and just who this Exterminator was.

"Hasn't raced since last July. Never been over six furlongs."

"He's been looking good in his trials..."

"But the Derby is about class. Class tells every time."

Exterminator's odds at post time of nearly 30-1 would have likely been much higher had it not been for his trials and the support of the Binghamton crowd, which came anyway with or without Sun Briar running. Kilmer himself put forty-five dollars on his horse. Henry McDaniel laid down two hundred dollars for favored War Cloud.

Aurum's and Jim Heffering's withdrawals left eight contestants to run in the mud. War Cloud remained the heavy favorite due to his trials, while local money poured in to back Kenneth Alexander's Escoba, trained by Kentuckian John S. Ward. Fans were still talking about Escoba's 1918 debut on May 1, when he put his nose on the ground at the break but was gaining on the two older horses ahead of him at the finish. Then on Monday, he won the nine-furlong Derby Trial at Lexington after which he drilled another furlong to post the Derby distance in 2:06. "...the horse that beats him will get the money," Ward predicted. Exterminator remained the longest shot on the board at 29.60-1. (Incidentally, Derby Day 1918 registered its first half-million-dollar betting handle figure, $525,648. The $161,565 bet on the Derby alone was another record.)

The field lined up behind the barrier with Escoba on the inside and the filly Viva America, who would win the Kentucky Oaks a few days later, to his right. Exterminator would break from number five. William Sanford Knapp had mixed feelings as he maneuvered the big gelding into position. He recalled McDaniel giving him a thumbs-up in the paddock. "Hurry home, Bill. You're on the best horse." Still, this was Knapp's first Derby, and he was supposed to be on Sun Briar.

At thirty, "Big Bill" wasn't much taller than the four feet, ten inches he reached at age thirteen. Born

in 1888 near the Hawthorne racetrack outside of Chicago where his father broke yearlings, Knapp was exercising runners by the time he was ten and competing at thirteen.

Atop Exterminator, he glanced at the horse directly to his left; War Cloud was antsy as usual, but Johnny Loftus sat him cool and calm. Loftus was a Derby veteran, having ridden in four and winning on board George Smith in 1916. Loftus and Knapp avoided each other's glances as riders do before a race. Neither could know then how interwoven their destinies would be a year later.

There were no starting gates in 1918, nor the open-ended stalls that debuted at Churchill Downs in 1930. The horses were lined up behind a net webbing stretched across the track. When the starter released the webbing, it catapulted up and out of the way. Much jostling took place behind the barrier then, but it took starter Dade only two minutes to get eight heads facing front. He released the net and shouted, "Come on!"

Viva America won the scramble to the lead and cleared her closest rival by more than a length as she zipped the opening quarter in :24 1/5. Sewell Combs followed on her heels, and Escoba on his. Loftus still had his hands full with War Cloud, who was trying to run up on the heels of horses in front of him. Exterminator was fifth as Knapp sat high and motion-less, looking capable of moving up anytime he chose.

The half-mile went by in :49 1/5, with Escoba beginning to close on the filly. Between the half-mile and three-quarters markers, Exterminator started "moving like he meant business..."

Coming out of the backstretch, Escoba replaced Viva America, who would finish third. Knapp lowered his seat and Exterminator moved with a rush that swept him to the lead, but Escoba wasn't about to concede the issue. Only in the last seventy yards did Exterminator reach down for another gear and draw out to win by a length. His time was an inconsequen-tial 2:10 4/5.

The crowd was partly subdued. So unexpected was Exterminator's victory that a local reporter was told by his editor to "sober up," when he submitted his story by phone. Turf writer William Frederick thought it as big "a surprise as ever sprung on a Derby day crowd."

And from Walter Pearce: "The unexpected happened. It is more than probable that quite a few of those in attendance at the Derby did not know that Exterminator was even a starter..." [3]

The report provided by Thomas Rust Underwood has gone down in racing lore.

"The clouds just wouldn't roll by.

"First rain fell to make the scene of the Kentucky Derby muddy.

"Then Exterminator dropped from them to win the event.

"Two weeks ago Willis Sharpe Kilmer, owner of Exterminator, made excuses for purchasing him from J. C. Milam, saying he only bought the gelding as a 'work' horse to make Sun Briar extend himself.

"Today, Exterminator is crowned king of the thoroughbred world."

Cal Milam kept the sale of Exterminator in perspective. Although Milam was increasingly impressed by the gelding and was prepared to run him in the Derby himself, Exterminator was an investment. "...when Willis Sharpe Kilmer made me an offer of $15,000 for him...it was the old story of 'a bird in the hand is worth two in the bush'…and incidentally, I have a few tickets on him at juicy odds in my pocket which I have not had a chance to cash." [4]

As for his nominating the gelding to the Derby back when Exterminator was a poor sight, Milam smiled. "An old trick I learned from John E. Madden, smartest horseman I've ever known. I went to work for him when I came here as a kid from Alabama. Having a colt eligible for the race helps sell him. Henry McDaniel wasn't going to buy Exterminator until I told him I thought so much of him I had put him in the Derby. It works." [5]

Even McDaniel was mildly surprised. "When I entered him in the Derby, I thought he stood a good chance, but knowing that he was racing against the crack three-year-olds of the American turf, I did not consider him a certainty by any means. I always thought, however, that he stood an excellent chance." [6] Which makes one wonder why he bet on War Cloud.

Willis Kilmer was giddy, as if he had been indulging in his Swamp Root, and making him a bit loose-tongued. "You must excuse me from talking, as I am too happy to know what I am saying. Gee, but it is great to win a Derby. I am delighted that I purchased

Exterminator. He is sure a great horse, and he can have anything in Binghamton. The same goes double for Jockey Knapp and Trainer McDaniel."

No one missed the fact he was singing a new tune. Suddenly, the decision to buy Exterminator and enter him in the Derby was of his own making. "I sent Sun Briar to Louisville last February to be trained for this race along with Nelsweep," he said, "but as the race got close, I saw that neither of them was ready...I then scurried about to get a worthy representative for the Derby, the price being of secondary consideration, and when I happened upon Exterminator I surely made a lucky strike. Sun Briar made a name for himself as a 2-year-old...and Exterminator is right in line with him when it comes to my estimation of the two horses." [7]

McDaniel held his tongue, appeased somewhat at the time by a thousand dollar bonus. A like amount went to Knapp. As for the race, Knapp said Exterminator's move in the last sixteenth of a mile "...certainly showed that he had a lot of heart. You can talk about game horses, but that old boy is there with the stamina. Right after his last workout with Sun Briar, Mr. McDaniel said that he believed he would win the Derby and when he threw me up on him today he told me...I was on the best horse..." [8]

Not everyone was impressed, however. Turf writer Charles Elmer Railey wrote that Exterminator "is not a high class horse, and his winning the Derby was a fluke. He belongs to the overnight handicaps and is worth about $3,500." [9]

Willis Kilmer's euphoria had worn off by the next day. Once again he was a man whose dislike for his own horse is one of racing's richest stories. Despite the winning purse of $14,700 — less the amount going to the Red Cross — and the forty-five dollar wager that parlayed into a little more than $1,346, Kilmer appeared sadder that it was not Sun Briar's victory, evidenced in this telegram he sent to the *Binghamton Press*:

"Exterminator, the horse I bought to work with Sun Briar, won the Derby. If Sun Briar had started, he would have won by five lengths, making Sun Briar first and Exterminator second in the Derby. Sun Briar always beat Exterminator by about five lengths every time they worked together."

Accompanying the telegram, and barely longer,

was Kilmer's own write-up of the race, and it repeat-ed much of what was in the telegram. Since the *Press* wasn't published on Sundays, the story appeared in the Monday edition. On the back page.

Just where Willis Kilmer probably wanted it.

EXTERMINATOR

CHAPTER 5

"Saratoga will be the grand annual meeting"

T he main threat to American racing in 1918 was whether the sport should be suspended for the duration of the war. Officials from North American tracks met in early summer, and all but those from Canada agreed that they could best serve the cause by remaining open. "If it were detrimental to the welfare of the country," said Aqueduct's president James Shevlin, "I would be one of the first to close the gates of Aqueduct."

Shevlin was right. Probably more money was raised for Liberty and War Bonds at racetracks than at any other sporting events. Owners donated winning purses, among them Philip A. Clark, who handed over Dunboyne's $23,360 Futurity Stakes check. The sport was also "providing desirable horses for military purposes," Shevlin reminded. Unfortunately, too many young horses were being gelded for one reason or another. And geldings can't reproduce.

So, in early August Matt Winn announced that geldings would be barred from running in the Kentucky Derby. "This great classic," he said, "which in the past few years has come to be regarded as the greatest of all events of the American turf...will continue to offer a $15,000 purse, [but] geldings will be tabooed. The government needs thoroughbred stallions in great numbers for the work of getting military horses." The timing of the announcement was fortuitous for Exterminator and maybe a bit ironic. Winn swore to his last days that Exterminator was the greatest all-around racehorse he ever saw.

By mid-summer of 1918, one and a half-million American horses, mostly Thoroughbreds, and mules had been shipped to Europe and with those provided by the Allies, an estimated five million animals were on the Western Front and more were needed. Said one American officer over there, "If we had a hundred guns for every German gun, and a hundred shells for every German shell, and our supply of horses gave out, the Allies could not win the war." [1]

World War I was still a horse-and-mule war. They pulled artillery caissons, carried supplies, and hauled munitions. Tanks had only recently appeared and were still lumbering things susceptible to frequent breakdowns. "Motors cannot cross fields ploughed with shells and soaked with rain..." said another officer. "The service of the horse in this war is beyond computation..." [2]

An anti-gelding movement had been growing even before the war, going under the guise of "betterment of the breed." Handicapper Walter S. Vosburgh said the Latonia Jockey Club's decision to ban geldings from Latonia Derbys beginning with the next year's renewal was "a step in the right direction. If we had more such events the turf would be on a sounder basis and we would have stouter and better horses." Paradoxically, the horse with the stoutest heart over the next five years was a gelding.

In the meantime, both Exterminator and Sun Briar were struggling. Following the Derby, Exterminator finished second in the Turf and Field Handicap at Belmont Park and the $10,000-added Latonia Derby on June 22. Sun Briar fared even worse, finishing sixth in the

Stuyvesant Handicap and Withers Stakes. Neither started again until the Saratoga meeting in August.

When George Washington first viewed the ramshackle huts clustered around High Rock Spring back in late July of 1783, he told friends accompanying him that there should be a national resort at these springs. Being a Virginian, and an accomplished horseman, he might have envisioned a racecourse. Eighty-one years later, Saratoga Race Course opened on August 2, 1864, to ten thousand fans, inaugurating a new track and an enduring classic, the Travers Stakes. One excited observer penned the following year, "By and by we shall have our Ascots, and Derbys, and Leger days, and Saratoga will be the grand annual meeting." [3]

A new racing surface greeted horsemen for the 1918 meeting. Track superintendent Billy Myer and his crew had replaced some two feet of old topsoil with fresh dirt, had installed a new drainage system, and had harrowed, rolled, and raked the new surface. Now all that was needed was a good rain. Right on cue, the track repelled a hard overnight shower on July 29.

Myer hadn't allowed horses to work on the new track until July 23, about a week before opening day.

Until then, horses galloped at Horse Haven, a former trotting track across Union Avenue. The next day, Myer loaned New York journalist John I. Day his "calico pony" and asked him to tour the track. The pony took some time to negotiate it, but "real racehorses were tearing off eighths of a mile in eleven seconds," Day wrote.

Other trainers who examined the track over the next few days agreed that Saratoga was the best in the country and predicted that a lot of records would fall during the meeting. After watching two-year-olds go four furlongs in :46, trainer John S. Ward said: "Watch the figures they'll hang out here before the meeting is over."

This preoccupation with speed was part of a recent trend to replace deep cushiony surfaces with harder, faster ones. In 1877 Ten Broeck became the first to crack the 1:40 mile, with 1:39 3/4, then it was twenty-four years before Brigadier broke 1:38 by a tick in 1901. In a special race against the clock in 1890, Salvator was timed in 1:35 1/2, but it came on a straight course. By 1918 most times in competition were in the low 1:37s, but more frequently times in the 1:36s were being clocked. And as the country's best gallopers arrived at Saratoga, everyone wondered which of the big-name

runners would hang up new numbers.

Certainly Eternal and Billy Kelly, the leading juveniles, would be among them. Sun Briar would be also
if he recovered his 1917 form, or Johren, winner of
five straight, including the Belmont Stakes and the
Suburban Handicap. Or maybe the great Roamer, who
was coming in off consecutive wins in the Empire City
and Mount Vernon handicaps, would make history.
Had there been a popularity contest, Andrew Miller's
seven-year-old gelding would have won it drawing
away. "Just wait until Roamer gets here," a veteran
groom was overheard saying. "That old horse is going
to run around this track in nothing at all when he once
gets started." [4]

Roamer was just fifteen hands, two inches, but his
breeding stirred every quixotic heart. His sire, Knight
Errant, was the teaser stallion on the Paris, Kentucky,
farm of Colonels E.F. Clay and Catesby Woodford.
Romantics might call it true love; but, clinically speak-
ing, primal instinct spurred Knight Errant supposedly
to jump a fence to be with a blind, former claimer
named Rose Tree II. The result of this forbidden tryst
was Roamer, foaled in 1911 and one of the great cam-

paigners of the early twentieth century.

First-timers to Saratoga stood in awe of the grand-stand, which was nearly as long as two football fields, its slate Victorian roof changing hues during the passage of an afternoon. Trimmed in dark red and dark bottle-green, with three pointed steeples in the center and another at each end of the steeply sloping roof, each topped with a gilded finial, the structure reflected the best of Gottfried Walbaum's tenure as owner during the end of the nineteenth century.

In the traditional opening day stakes races, W.F. Polson's Billy Kelly won the Flash, equaling the track record of 1:05 3/5 for five and a half furlongs. Roamer beat Cudgel for his third Saratoga Handicap in a new standard of 2:02 1/5 for ten furlongs. In an allowance the next day, Sun Briar finished second to Polymelian, who won in track-record time of 1:10 3/5 for six furlongs.

On the meeting's first Saturday, Billy Kelly ran again and won the United States Hotel Stakes under 127 pounds. Exterminator made his Saratoga debut in the fourth race, the mile and three-sixteenths Kenner Stakes. With top weight of 129 pounds, and spotting his four rivals up to fifteen, he wore down Tippity

Witchet in the stretch, but was too late to catch Enfilade, who equaled the American record of 1:56 3/5. Just three days into the meet, six records had been broken or equaled.

On Monday, Star Realm lowered Billy Kelly's recent standard for five and a half furlongs to 1:05 2/5. Also that day, Corn Tassel inked a new Saratoga mile standard of 1:37 1/5, which Sun Briar lowered by a full second in the Delaware Handicap on Tuesday. Some clockers caught him in 1:36 flat.

On August 7 Star Hampton beat Billy Kelly, toting 133 pounds, in the Albany Handicap. Canadian horseman J.K.L. Ross had been eyeing Billy Kelly for several days. The son of Dick Welles was small and said to be homely, but he had heart and loads of talent. Before the day was over, Ross had added him to his already star-studded barn for $27,500. W.F. Polson realized a tidy profit, having paid only $1,500 for the gelding at the 1917 yearling sales. Billy Kelly promptly won the Sanford Memorial Stakes by eight lengths under 130 pounds and the Grab Bag Handicap six days later. He was to have run in the Adirondack Handicap on August 28, but Walter Vosburgh slapped the two-year-old with 140 pounds and Ross put Billy Kelly on a south-bound train.

Meanwhile, yearlings for the 1918 sales had been arriving. Unloaded from the train terminal on West Circular Street, they were paraded through quiet and shady neighborhoods. Most went to the yearling barns at Horse Haven, but August Belmont's lot from his Nursery Stud in Lexington were led to his private facility, a stable and seven-furlong training track complex just south of the main track. Over the next few days a steady stream of prospective buyers toured the barns.

Saratoga's first-ever night auction was held by Fasig-Tipton on August 5, with another on the 8th. But the auction that would make history was held on August 17, Travers Day. About noon, August Belmont's yearlings went on the Powers-Hunter Company block beneath the elms in the Saratoga paddock. Samuel Riddle, of Glen Riddle, Pennsylvania, won the bidding at five thousand dollars for a handsome chestnut son of Fair Play from the Belmont consignment. Riddle also purchased ten other youngsters. Those ten were blanks, he said years later. "The eleventh was Man o' War."

Later in the afternoon, a record crowd of some

twenty thousand watched the Travers Stakes. Only four went to the barrier: Exterminator, Andy Schuttinger up, and Sun Briar, with Bill Knapp, coupled in the betting as the close to even-money favorites; Johren; and War Cloud. Sun Briar caught Johren in the last twenty yards and won by a head in 2:03 1/5. While it didn't threaten Roamer's track record, it was a stakes record. Exterminator forced War Cloud wide in an incident on the first turn, taking both out of serious contention.

In the meeting's third week, the track just seemed to get quicker. On August 21, Roamer raced against Salvator's twenty-eight-year-old world-record mile of 1:35 1/2 and knocked it down to 1:34 4/5. Moreover, while Salvator had set his record with the aid of two pace horses over Monmouth Park's straight course, Roamer had another horse with him only for a few yards after the break and, breaking from the mile chute that merged onto the track on the clubhouse turn, had one full turn and part of another. It was an amazing display for the seven-year-old. One of the first to offer Andrew Miller congratulations was Salvator's aging trainer, Matt Byrnes. "You have a great horse," Byrnes said. "I hope his record stands as long as Salvator's did." [5]

Not to be outdone, Willis Kilmer announced a few days later that Sun Briar would race against the clock on Thursday, August 29, if the track was fast. "If not he will go another day, and I will send him over the distance in private, if the trial cannot be made before the close of the meeting." Sun Briar had been scheduled to run in the Saratoga Cup on closing day Saturday. But Kilmer said he preferred to "have the colt make a record mile than to win the cup, but this would be more for my own satisfaction, to know how fast he can go, than any other reason." [6]

For a race against the clock to be official, it had to be run under the auspices of a recognized meeting and sanctioned by racing officials. Edward Hotaling, in his book *They're Off! Horse Racing at Saratoga*, mentions that Roamer's mile attempt would be the "last mile record against time..."

It rained Thursday. And Friday. And on Saturday, closing day. Sun Briar's attempt wouldn't be made until after the meeting's close.

Meanwhile, Exterminator nearly registered his first win at the Spa on Friday. Carrying top weight of 115 pounds in the Cohoes Handicap and conceding up to thirteen pounds to older horses, Exterminator was in full stride in the stretch when four-year-old Ticket, running on the outside, cut across in front of him and knocked him back to fourth. Exterminator had enough grit to claim at least third place. A foul claim against the winner, Ticket, was disallowed.

Saratoga's meeting closed with the traditional Hopeful Stakes and Saratoga Cup. Eternal won the former, and in the Cup, three-year-old Johren led every muddy step of the mile and three-quarters to beat Roamer. It had been a meeting unparalleled for speed — nineteen records broken or equaled, including three world records. But there was one other event.

On September 11, with the aid of two pace horses, Sun Briar turned a mile in 1:34 flat. It was unofficial, but brilliant, and more than anything else stamped him as one of the Golden Age's best gallopers.

Meanwhile, across Union Avenue at Horse Haven, Riddle's trainer, Louis Feustel, attempted to break Man o' War, but it was a near-constant battle of wills. The colt was Fair Play's son, a firestorm in a bridle.

As for Exterminator, his time would come.

CHAPTER 6

A Legend In The Making

H enry McDaniel didn't feel like he had anything to prove as a trainer; his record over the past thirty-plus years spoke for itself. So he was naturally stung by talk that he had mismanaged Sun Briar's earlier problems. He could have reminded them about Forest.

Forest was a promising but chronically lame colt owned by M.E. Clark of Louisville. Clark was one of those less glamorous owners. He owned a "shoestring" stable that usually had to rob from the month's grocery money to pay for horse feed and vet bills. He owned two horses. Forest was the better one. The colt had the potential, if he could just get the right handling. So when a seventeen-year-old kid with a brand-new trainer's license and a respected last name came along, Clark hired him for a paltry twelve dollars a month. Even in 1885 it was hardly a living wage.

"I had no expensive habits," McDaniel explained years later. He identified Forest's problem as a blind splint (an inflammation of the ligament that joins the splint bone to the cannon bone), treated it, and sent the colt out to win five races, the last four in a row. McDaniel's salary was doubled. The Hollywood-esque story ended all too soon, however. In a freak accident the next year, Forest broke a leg. Clark folded. McDaniel moved on.

Henry McDaniel's father, Colonel David McDaniel, was one of the top trainers of the post-Civil War era. He was the first to saddle three consecutive winners of the Belmont Stakes, beginning with Harry Bassett in 1871. Frank McCabe repeated the feat in the late 1880s; then it was nearly a century before Woody Stephens went two better, winning five in a row in the 1980s.

"I was practically born on a race-track," Henry recalled, "one owned by my father…at Seacaucus, New Jersey, and this most interesting event occurred on September 10, 1867." Henry was galloping his father's horses as soon as he was big enough. Henry and a younger brother, Will, were the second generation of the famed "McDaniel Confederacy" that dominated the sport for several decades. Will's son, D.R. "Puddin" McDaniel, conditioned some nice horses himself, including the crack runner Vanderpool.

It was this McDaniel legacy that had prompted Clark to hire Henry. McDaniel's first big break came when he was hired by Elias "Lucky" Baldwin for whom he saddled the likes of Emperor of Norfolk and Rey el Santa Anita, the latter handing mighty Domino his first loss in the 1894 American Derby. Other top stables followed, right up to 1916 and the employ of Willis Kilmer. The Kilmer-McDaniel relationship was stormy; Kilmer at times took control of the horses' conditioning. His decision, in the latter half of 1918, to control Sun Briar caused the first rift.

After Saratoga, Sun Briar went home, and McDaniel took the stable to Laurel Park, located about halfway between Baltimore and Washington, D.C. It was October. Cool mornings had replaced the saturating heat of the coast. The war seemed to be coming to an end. But now, there was a new horror. J.K.M. Ross, the son of the Canadian horseman, remembered it well. "...this was the year and the month when the terrible influenza epidemic which raged through Europe

and America was at its height. Places of amusement were shut down everywhere, including Laurel. For a week there was no racing there..."

The virus, later identified as Type A, or Spanish flu, struck first in September at an army base near Boston. The second outbreak originated among the multi-national forces in France. Wounded and furloughed men carried the virus home, spreading it throughout Europe. By the time the great influenza pandemic of 1918-1919 ran its course, some twenty million people worldwide had died, between five- and six-hundred thousand in the United States alone.

When Laurel did open, Exterminator began the markedly improved last half of his three-year-old campaign. In five trips to the post there in October, he won three, beginning with an easy score in the Artillery Liberty Bond Purse at a mile and one-sixteenth. Four days later he wired a classier bunch to win the Carrolton Handicap at the same distance, barely missing the track standard. The nine-furlong Washington Handicap on the 12th was his third start in eight days, and he finished third behind cracks Midway and Cudgel. Two weeks later he led from start to finish in the nine-furlong Ellicott City Handicap, and in his last start at Laurel, he gave four-year-old Midway scale weight and drove him to a head in the National Handicap.

It was just a jaunt then from Laurel to Baltimore, where Exterminator started twice at Pimlico, "Old Hilltop." Many tracks have lakes in their infields. Pimlico had a hill, around which, for some reason, the track had been built back in 1870. It was a nice touch, except that spectators in the lower grandstand couldn't see part of the backstretch action. The prominence was leveled in 1938, but the place lovingly remains "Old Hilltop."

Exterminator galloped to within a tick of the ten-furlong track record in the Pimlico Autumn Handicap on November 6. Five days later, the world's agony ended at Compiegne, France, with the signing of the armistice. More than eight and a half-million were dead on both sides, twenty-one-million-plus wounded. For most of the million and a half horses and mules that America sent to war, there were no parades, no medals, just quick pyres.

In the Bowie Handicap on November 12, Pimlico

fans were afforded a rare opportunity to see three Kentucky Derby winners in one race: George Smith (1916), Omar Khayyam (1917), and Exterminator, who gave weight to some of his elders. They finished in that order, with George Smith recording a new track record of 2:31 4/5 for the mile and a half.

Exterminator won both season-ending starts at Latonia. On November 23 he hinted of things to come as he led every step of the Latonia Cup's demanding two and a quarter miles to nose out Beaverkill. It was Johnny Loftus' first ride on the gelding, and the two meshed like they had grown up together. They repeated the feat five days later in the Thanksgiving Handicap.

McDaniel's patience had paid off. Exterminator had won six of his last nine starts and seven of fifteen for the year with earnings of $36,147. Johren was the consensus champion three-year-old on the basis of his top earnings of $49,156. In the juvenile division, Eternal beat out Billy Kelly in the John R. McLean Memorial on October 28 to finish with six wins in eight starts and $56,137. But Billy Kelly's record of fourteen wins in seventeen starts was brilliant. Among the senior set, four-year-old Cudgel led with earnings of $33,826 in nine wins out of seventeen starts.

Exterminator wintered at Oaklawn Park in Hot Springs, Arkansas, and won both of his starts there in March, the Hotel Como and New Era handicaps, each with different riders. Returning to Lexington was like going back home. He won the Ben Ali Handicap at a mile and one-sixteenth on May 1, with John Morys up, his third new rider in as many starts, and the ten-furlong Camden Handicap under 132 pounds a week later for his sixth straight victory.

Willis Kilmer had a gelding named Frogtown in the Kentucky Derby, and he hoped lightning would strike twice. But against the likes of Eternal and Billy Kelly, Frogtown was a fish out of water and finished eleventh. Sir Barton won the roses and later the Preakness and Belmont stakes. The term "Triple Crown" hadn't been coined as yet, but Sir Barton was still the first.

Exterminator was usually willing to run wherever he was placed. But in a mile purse at Churchill Downs on May 15, his will contradicted McDaniel's, which was to keep him off the pace. After fighting Morys' strong hold for six furlongs, Exterminator tired to fin-

ish second. A week later he was allowed to run his own race and wired the Galt House Handicap field to win by five lengths under 134 pounds in the mud. Two days was a bit too soon to carry that impost again over a mile and a quarter, and he finished third in the Kentucky Handicap.

In the meantime, Sun Briar, who had been bred to eighteen mares earlier in the spring, was being primed for a return. "He'll be ready by Saratoga," Kilmer informed the media. When the rest of the stable arrived in New York late in May, Sun Briar was under tack, galloping off some excess flab. Admiring fans agreed he never looked better.

"Sun Briar is a superb specimen of the thoroughbred race horse," one journalist from the *New York Herald* wrote. "He is the color of old San Domingo mahogany, stands about 15.3 hands high, and looks as much like an equine gamecock as any horse the writer ever saw..." The reporter described the ringbones as "pronounced" in his ankles, but Sun Briar's veterinarian, Dr. R.W. McCully, assured they had never given him trouble and, in fact, had never even felt a firing iron.

When Exterminator threw in baffling fifth-place finishes in the Suburban Handicap on June 7 at Belmont Park and the Excelsior Handicap a week later at Jamaica, tongues began to wag that he lacked substance. McDaniel knew better and put him up until Saratoga.

Then, suddenly, Kilmer moved Sun Briar's schedule up. He wired McDaniel on Wednesday, July 9, instructing him to get the colt ready for the Empire City Handicap. Roamer was entered in that race, and Kilmer had been waiting for this opportunity since last August. But Roamer, winless in four starts this year, had already been withdrawn. The eight-year-old gelding was still sound, though, and owner Andrew Miller decided later to give him "another chance to win a race..."

The two finally met on Friday, July 11, in the six-furlong Domino Handicap at Aqueduct. The match-up appeared one-sided. The old man nearing the end of his career against a youngster half his age and at his peak. So in an effort to even things up a bit, handicapper Walter Vosburgh handed Sun Briar 130 pounds, sixteen more than Roamer's impost.

He was the Roamer of old, beating Sun Briar to the wire by three-quarters of a length. It was his only win that year and his last hurrah. Following a second in the Yonkers Handicap on July 26, Miller retired him to Arthur Schott's farm in New Jersey. On New Year's Day, 1920, hours after Miller suffered a fatal heart attack, Roamer slipped on ice in his paddock, broke a leg, and was put down.

Following his defeat by Roamer, Sun Briar finished third in the mile Mount Vernon Handicap at Empire City racetrack. Although Lucullite was the clear winner, everyone agreed that Sun Briar would have been second had Johnny Loftus not allowed the Kilmer colt to drift off the rail on the turn for home, thus giving Old Rosebud room to slip through for second place. The stewards called in Loftus, said to be headstrong and cocky.

Loftus had a record of ride infractions and was even yanked off A.K. Macomber's mounts when he failed to follow instructions on War Cloud. It was Loftus who was aboard Man o' War in the colt's only defeat in the 1919 Sanford Memorial Stakes. Yet Sam Riddle never blamed him. As for the race just lost with Sun Briar,

Loftus apologized and everyone let it go at that.

Their reputations sullied, Exterminator and Sun Briar were loaded onto a train in Yonkers and shipped north up the Hudson River Valley for Saratoga. The best horses were scheduled to be there: Cudgel, Lucullite, Sir Barton, Billy Kelly, and Purchase. And that two-year-old, undefeated firestorm, Man o' War, who opened his Saratoga campaign winning the United States Hotel Stakes on August 2 for his sixth win.

The Kilmer duo started on August 5 in the Delaware Handicap, the race in which Sun Briar had set the American record for a mile the year before. The track was lightning fast, fueling speculation that the colt would break his own mark. But it was the crack race mare Fairy Wand, with Sun Briar breathing down her neck, who equaled Sun Briar's record. Exterminator finished a length behind his barn mate, but it appeared to many that he hadn't been persevered with in the stretch. It became even more apparent the next time out.

Fairy Wand tried to repeat in the nine-furlong Champlain Handicap on the 9th, but Sun Briar won in a track record 1:50 flat. Exterminator, after being

under a snug hold to the far turn, moved so easily into contention in the stretch that he would have caught Sun Briar had not Loftus gathered him in again, while Knapp had to ride the colt vigorously to maintain a length margin.

Even the chart's trip notes indicated that Exterminator was "...not hard ridden in the final eighth." A journalist for *The New York Times* said Loftus appeared to pull up "with Exterminator after the other contenders had been beaten off in the stretch drive..." And in the *Herald*: "Exterminator might have won this race if he had had to or if Mr. Kilmer had not declared to win with Sun Briar." Thomas F. "Doc" Marshall Sr., a longtime friend of Kilmer's, confirmed that jockeys were instructed to hold Exterminator back "so another favorite horse of his could win!"

Legal, according to the "rules of racing" of The Jockey Club of New York. Any owner with more than one entry in a race can declare to win with one of them, as long as the declaration is made at the weighing out and posted on the notice board.

Four days after the Champlain, Saratoga witnessed a shocker. In the Sanford Memorial, a race full of bad luck, Man o' War, with Johnny Loftus up, lost to Bill Knapp-ridden Upset. Man o' War redeemed his honor in the Grand Union Hotel Stakes on Saturday, August 23.

Man o' War didn't just beat Upset, he rubbed it in, galloping while the son of Whisk Broom II ran his heart out. In the next race on the card, a half-hour later, a great field promised a great show: Exterminator, Sun Briar, Cudgel, and two others. Unfortunately, the ending left a bad taste in everyone's mouth.

Johnny Loftus received his usual instructions — yield the outcome to Sun Briar. The latter laid just off Exterminator's early pace, then began his move. Dutifully Loftus began hauling in his mount, and Sun Briar rushed to the front on the far turn. This time, Earl Sande on Cudgel was anticipating these antics and had his mount running more forward than usual. With Exterminator geared down, Sande blew by him then overtook Sun Briar, who was tiring. Loftus tried to get his mount's momentum back, but by then Star Master had also passed him.

Sun Briar wouldn't start again at Saratoga, but

Exterminator went to the plate one more time in the Saratoga Cup.

A legend was in the making.

CHAPTER 7

"...the Abe Lincoln of race horses"

M ost of the hype prior to the 1919 Saratoga Cup focused on Sam Hildreth's three-year-old colt Purchase, for whom his owner had just recently turned down a record offer of $300,000. He had already beaten all the top runners in his division, so that by the end of August his potential meeting at even weight with Cudgel in the Saratoga Cup was the talk of the Spa.

"With a fast track Cudgel, War Pennant, Purchase, and possibly Eternal, will be among the starters," *The New York Times* reported. "Should it rain it is feared the race will be left to the mercy of Purchase, which runs well on any kind of track." It did rain and Cudgel was withdrawn. Exterminator wasn't even mentioned, but then a lack of respect was customary at this stage in his career.

Either due to the rain or Cudgel's absence, only

twenty thousand or so fans showed up, a small crowd for closing day. But with or without a Cudgel-Purchase match-up, Man o' War was running in the rich Hopeful Stakes, although the outcome was rather anticlimactic. If the fans thought the Saratoga Cup would end in a like manner for Purchase, they were sorely mistaken.

The light rain of the past two days turned into a torrential downpour right before the Hopeful and fell even harder when the Cup field approached the starter. Only three horses showed up: the mud-loving Purchase, winner of the Huron Handicap four days earlier; Exterminator, with Andy Schuttinger in the irons; and J.J. Maher's The Trump, ridden by Phil Musgrave. The rain was falling so hard that starter Mars Cassidy dispensed with the barrier and sent the horses off from a walk-up.

Years later, Sam Hildreth talked about the faith he had in Purchase that day. "Exterminator was a Hindoo over a route and a bear in the mud," he said, "but I was never more confident of anything than I was that I would win that race." [1]

But Exterminator went straight to the front and never looked back. He seemed to skim over the mud like a dragonfly on a pond. When he turned into the stretch, Schuttinger asked him to put the race away, and Exterminator turned it on. At this point Bill Knapp, no longer Kilmer's contract rider, gave Purchase a smack, without getting much of a response. When he raised the whip a second time, it slipped from his hand.

Foul! Purchase's backers howled. Hildreth blamed the finish on the loss of the whip. "...but not so," reported the *New York Herald*. "Exterminator won on his merits. Purchase was beaten when the whip was lost." Indeed a dozen whips would not have changed the outcome. Exterminator ran to perfection, and his time of 2:58 at the end of fourteen furlongs equaled the track record.

Among the scores of reporters who flocked to the Kilmer barn afterward, one journalist for the *New York Herald* lingered after the others had gone. He wanted to get to know Exterminator. He wanted his readers to know him.

McDaniel unfastened the stall webbing so the reporter could get a look at the grand gelding. Exterminator stood in his stall munching from a feed bin in a far corner. He turned his head to look at his visitors, then resumed his meal. The reporter was struck by his size, the powerful sloping shoulders that anchored the long, clean legs. Some observers likened Exterminator's lanky leanness to a greyhound, but this reporter was reminded of a human counterpart...our sixteenth president.

"...the Abe Lincoln of race horses," he wrote. "He is 16.2 hands high, and he has the tall, ungainly, gangling form of an equine backwoodsman, with the amiable, affectionate disposition of a family buggy horse.

"Exterminator isn't old...but he is hollow above the eyes like an old horse, and is such a homely, awkward, dejected looking figure when standing around without anything to do with those long legs of his that anybody would be excusable for guessing he was older..."

McDaniel beckoned to Exterminator, and the gelding moved to where Henry stood and rubbed his head on the trainer's shoulder. They had a genuine mutual affection for each other. The *Herald* reporter asked McDaniel about Sun Briar and the trainer had nothing but praise for the colt's appearance, "...one of the most perfect specimens of the English race horse he has seen, but somehow the conversation soon drifts to the chestnut gelding, and then there is enthusiasm in his speech as he tells you Exterminator is the most honest, generous, admirable horse he ever trained.

"Some of the best horsemen in the country have been a long time learning to take Exterminator seriously." Then McDaniel assured his visitor the gelding was improving and respect would come.

The gelding's next start was to have been the $10,000-added Jockey Club Stakes at Belmont Park on September 13, a new weight-for-age at a mile and a half. But not all the anti-gelding sentiment had ended with the armistice, and some horsemen had sought to keep unsexed males out of this event.

"There are too few of these races," an anonymous journalist penned in the *Times*, "but the encouragement the breeders received from the Government during the war...to keep the horses in this country up to the standards maintained in Europe, has created new interest." The decision to allow geldings to run angered some horsemen.

"The Jockey Club Stakes has been left open to geldings," the journalist lamented, "despite the fact that it aims directly to aid the breeders, but there is always the hope among horsemen that an entire horse will win. There was some regret expressed over the victory of Exterminator in the Saratoga Cup because a gelding beat an entire horse."

The article appeared after Kilmer had ordered McDaniel to take the stable to Havre de Grace in Maryland, bypassing New York's fall meetings, but the wealthy sportsman was well aware of the sentiment. Although Exterminator was now eligible to run, Kilmer might have been irked enough to skip the Jockey Club Stakes.

Havre de Grace, affectionately known as "the Graw," had opened in August 1912. The track lay about two miles south of the town of the same name and some thirty-six miles equally from Baltimore and Wilmington. The track's nearly quarter-mile home-stretch was overlooked by an iron grandstand that seated six thousand.

That grandstand was full when the Graw's seventeen-day meeting began on September 11. The marquee event, the inaugural running of the Harford County Handicap at a mile and seventy yards, was advertised as "...a championship contest in itself."

Among the entries were Exterminator, Sun Briar, Sir Barton, Billy Kelly, The Porter, and Cudgel. "This race will settle the rivalry between Cudgel and Sun Briar, which began when the great campaigner from the Ross Stable defeated Sun Briar in the Merchants' and Citizens' Handicap at Saratoga." The writer failed to mention that three horses, including Exterminator, beat Sun Briar in that race.

But then the skies opened up, resulting in a mass exodus until only The Porter, Exterminator, and three others started. Exterminator carried 125 pounds and conceded four to The Porter. Not a tall order for this horse, but he didn't look like his old self, and The Porter outran him in the stretch to win by four lengths. Eleven days later, Exterminator held off Cudgel's patented late run to win the Republic Purse, equaling the Havre de Grace track record of 1:45 for a mile and one-sixteenth.

The Republic was a prep for the nine-furlong Havre de Grace Handicap five days later, a race that won Exterminator a multitude of new fans and a barnful of respect. In recounting the race's history of fielding good runners, Charles Hatton wrote, "Did a better field

Exterminator, affectionately known to his fans as "Old Bones," remains one of horse racing's most beloved figures.

McGee (top), sire of Exterminator, led the national sire list in 1922, the year his most famous son was at his peak. Exterminator's dam, Fair Empress (right), came from sturdy stock, including her sire, stakes winner Jim Gore (below). Jim Gore was a son of the 1881 Kentucky Derby winner Hindoo.

Lexington horseman J. Cal Milam (below on right with longtime
Lexington Herald publisher Desha Breckinridge) purchased
Exterminator as a yearling for $1,500 and raced the gelding at two.
Milam was perhaps better known as the owner of Merrick
(above with Milam in 1932), who lived to age thirty-eight.

Binghamton, New York, business-man Willis Sharpe Kilmer (right) made his money selling the cure-all "Swamp Root." The Kilmer Building where Swamp Root was manufactured still stands in Binghamton (bottom), as does Kilmer's house (below).

Due in part to Kilmer's irascible nature, Exterminator went through numerous trainer changes. Exterminator's first and next-to-last trainer for Kilmer was Henry McDaniel (right), who acquired the gelding for the owner prior to the 1918 Kentucky Derby. Another trainer was former jockey Bill Knapp (above), who had ridden Exterminator in the Derby and several other races.

In addition to Knapp, Exterminator part-nered with many jockeys during his long career. Three of his most regular riders were Albert Johnson (above), Charlie Fairbrother (right), and Bill Kelsay (below).

Exterminator and Kilmer's stable star Sun Briar (below,
Exterminator on outside) worked together in the weeks
leading up to the Kentucky Derby, but Sun Briar didn't
make the race. Kilmer reluctantly substituted Exterminator,
who surprised his owner with a victory (above).

In the 1919 Champlain Handicap at Saratoga (top), Sun Briar managed a length victory over stablemate Exterminator (second on rail), who was "not hard ridden" to the finish. At five in 1920, Exterminator captured ten stakes, including the Luke Blackburn Handicap (above) at Aqueduct.

Exterminator started five times during August 1920. Three of his outings were at Saratoga, including a runner-up effort to 1919 Triple Crown winner Sir Barton in the Saratoga Handicap (below) and an easy victory over Cleopatra in the Saratoga Cup (above).

Following his Saratoga Cup win, Exterminator traveled to Belmont Park where he narrowly won the Autumn Gold Cup (above). In 1921 the grand gelding took the Merchants' and Citizens' Handicap (below) at Saratoga over Mad Hatter (in white blinkers).

Mad Hatter (above) and Exterminator were perennial rivals and exchanged victories and placings on several occasions, but it seemed that Mad Hatter was chasing Exterminator more often than not (top).

Exterminator was under tight restraint as he held off Be Frank in an overnight handicap (below) at Belmont in June 1922. Later that summer, Exterminator held off the great Grey Lag to win the Brooklyn Handicap (left). Exterminator and Mad Hatter renewed their rivalry in the Saratoga Cup (above), and Exterminator prevailed to earn his fourth victory in the race.

Dispersal of

COURT MANOR STUD

IN
"Shenandoah Valley"
THE PROPERTY OF
THE LATE WILLIS SHARPE KILMER

COMPRISING

STALLIONS, WEANLINGS, BROODMARES, ETC.

AT THE FARM
(3 Miles South of)
NEW MARKET, VIRGINIA

ON

Wednesday, October 30, 1940

Sale Starts Promptly at 10:30 A. M.

• • •

FASIG-TIPTON COMPANY
604 Fifth Avenue   New York City
K. I. TRANTER, President

Kilmer had developed several farm properties over the years, including Court Manor Stud in Virginia. Upon his death in 1940, a dispersal sale was held there.

In 1941 Exterminator made a return to the track along with pony companion, Peanuts, to lead the post parade of the Exterminator Handicap at Pimlico.

Under the care of groom Mike Terry (above, holding the shank),
"Old Bones" aged gracefully and loved children.
Mrs. Willis Kilmer (below with a
twenty-eight-year-old Exterminator and
twenty-year-old Peanuts)
held birthday parties
for the old gelding.

Exterminator died at the age of thirty in 1945, two years after his old stablemate Sun Briar. Both are buried, along with the mare Suntica, in the LaFrance pet cemetery in Binghamton.

ever parade for a renewal of the Havre de Grace than that...in 1919?" In addition to Exterminator, who had 126 pounds, the field included the Ross entry of Cudgel, top weight with 129 pounds, and Sir Barton, whose 124-pound package was four over scale. The Canadian horseman had already enjoyed success in the two races just preceding the Havre with His Choice and Billy Kelly. Also in the field, The Porter, who last out had beaten Sir Barton in an allowance; Midway; Tippity Witchet; and two others. The Ross duo went off at odds-on, with Exterminator 10-1.

Straightaway, Sir Barton and Cudgel sandwiched the field, racing up to ten lengths apart, with the Triple Crown winner rattling along in :23 3/5, :47 1/5, 1:12 2/5, and a mile in 1:37 3/5. This was the Triple Crown winner's style, and he did it well enough that he had set an American record in the Belmont. This time, however, his legs grew heavy in the stretch. Meanwhile, Bill Knapp had settled Exterminator back in sixth and had orders to move when Cudgel moved. So when that five-year-old bay launched his attack on the far turn, Knapp called on his mount. "Stermy," as Hatton called Exterminator, was in full stride when he was cut off by a tiring horse and had to check sharply. He regained his momentum and was forced to check a second time. Cudgel went on out and appeared to be home free.

Most horses lose heart at this point, but what separates the truly great runners from the others may be that their hearts seem larger. Exterminator reached down for his, and it got him within a half-length of Cudgel, who had to run the nine furlongs in track-record time of 1:50.

The action moved to Laurel, where Exterminator won a prep for the October 11 Annapolis Handicap. In the latter, Thunderclap, receiving twenty pounds from Exterminator, was pushed to a new American record of 2:29 3/5 for the mile and a half. "...in a few more strides he (Exterminator) would have been the winner." [2]

Cudgel lacked his usual energy during his drive, and he finished well back in third.

On October 18 Exterminator's attempt to win a second Latonia Cup was hindered by his 134-pound impost, the mud, and a "duel" under wraps with Latonia Derby winner Be Frank for most of the two and a quarter miles. "They alternated in taking the lead," observed a *Times* writer, "but were running close together, so that it mattered little which was in front from time to time…Not until the last quarter of a mile did Be Frank have an advantage which counted for anything…" This was Exterminator's third start in fifteen days, and he tired with the additional twelve pounds. Knapp eased him in the final yards to finish second.

When Royce Rools, Cudgel, Mad Hatter, and Boniface all finished in front of him in the Bowie Handicap on November 8 for his third straight loss, talk circulated among fans and racing writers that Exterminator was over the hill. They were certainly surprised when he started again just five days later in the Pimlico Cup, another two and a quarter-miler.

Pimlico inaugurated the Cup that year and from a hundred nominations only three started: Exterminator, Royce Rools, and Woodtrap. This was Exterminator's fourth start in as many weeks and his second at eighteen furlongs. A burden for any other horse, but looking back, it was the quintessential race for Exterminator — distance, top weight, and mud.

In the meantime Sun Briar returned to his first competition since Saratoga in a six-furlong handicap at

Laurel on October 22. When a reporter for *The New York Times* asked McDaniel if he missed the "star" of the Kilmer stable, McDaniel snapped back, "No. I have a first-rate distance runner in Exterminator."

Sun Briar finished fourth and then closed his career running third in the Laurel Stakes on October 25. He was retired with a record of twenty-two starts, eight wins — all stakes and all but one coming at Saratoga — with nine placings and earnings of $74,355.

Just who was the better horse remained a hot topic for years. McDaniel once picked Sun Briar at distances up to a mile and a half. This is interesting, considering the colt never raced beyond ten furlongs and just once at that distance. On another occasion, McDaniel said Exterminator was the best horse he ever trained. Sun Briar was a brilliant racehorse and might have been the best miler of his time, but the racing public never got to see him in a fair competition with his stablemate since Kilmer declared to win with Sun Briar each time the two horses raced together.

In the Pimlico Cup, on yet another rainy day, Exterminator carried high weight of 121 pounds with Clarence Kummer up for the second time. Exterminator conceded sixteen pounds to Royce Rools and nineteen to Woodtrap, and he made hash of both. He led the race under a pull for ten furlongs, and with a half-mile to go, Kummer relaxed his hold. Royce Rools pulled within two in the stretch, but Exterminator turned him back as one would flick a bug off a table and drew off to win by four lengths in 4:13.

With this victory he was retired for the year, having won nine of twenty-one starts and earnings of $26,402, which topped the season for four-year-olds. He had raced at ten different tracks in four states, performed equally well on any surface, and carried weight. The end of 1919 ended part one of Exterminator's career. The Pimlico Cup was his fortieth start, eighteen of which he won.

It also temporarily ended McDaniel's relationship with Willis Kilmer. Henry would only say it was "a disagreement." But Kilmer is said to have boasted he "had made" McDaniel's career, and for the trainer, it was just one hole too many in an already leaky boat.

The next three years were collectively the peak of Exterminator's career and would define his place in history.

EXTERMINATOR

CHAPTER 8

Mr. Kilmer And Mr. Riddle

L ike J.K.M. Ross, sports historian Bob Moore was entranced with racing in what he called the "Golden Age," a period that began in 1908 and lasted three decades. Moore's favorite, however, was the twenties, which he referred to in his book, *Those Wonderful Days*, as the "Golden Decade." "The temptation to write of the great horses that ran over American tracks in the Golden Decade is great," he wrote, "but it shall be resisted. Just two shall be remembered, Exterminator and Man o' War. Any era which could boast these two was certainly favored by chance."

Racing enjoyed an unprecedented popularity in 1920. Man o' War raised the bar to new heights, and the veteran Exterminator began a period in his career the likes of which hasn't been equaled. Although separated in age by two years, these two warhorses were surely destined to meet on the battlefield.

They came close on a number of occasions, including running in races on the same day, May 29, 1920, at Belmont Park. It was Exterminator's first start of the season and Man o' War's second, having won the Preakness Stakes eleven days earlier. Shortly after four o'clock that afternoon, Man o' War demolished his two rivals in the Withers, running the mile in 1:35 4/5 and eclipsing Sun Briar's record. Some twenty-five minutes later, J. Simon Healy tightened the girth on Exterminator's saddle and boosted T. Davies into the irons for the Elmont Handicap, a $1,520 purse race at a mile and one-sixteenth.

When Kilmer hired him in late July 1918 to handle a few of his horses at Saratoga, Healy was operating a small public stable. The Elmont Handicap was his first time to send Exterminator to the post. Unraced for six months and conceding up to forty-one pounds to his rivals, the gelding was short by a neck to Alibi.

Man o' War and Exterminator remained at Belmont for their next starts, with different results. Against a single opponent, Man o' War won the mile and three-eighths Belmont Stakes by twenty lengths in 2:14 1/5, three and one-fifth seconds faster than the old standard. Only Count Fleet in 1943 and Secretariat in 1973 ever won the Belmont by a wider margin. A week earlier on June 5, Exterminator had run in the Suburban Handicap, finishing third behind the year's Kentucky Derby winner Paul Jones and J.K.L. Ross' five-year-old Boniface.

Exterminator's two losses did not faze Kilmer, who was giddy about Sun Briar's success in the breeding shed. From the moment he purchased Sun Briar, Kilmer had looked beyond the colt's career on the track to the one in the breeding shed. He wanted to achieve eminence as a breeder with Sun Briar, the undisputed sovereign of Sun Briar Court, as the foundation. Now he had the results of those first seeds. From the eighteen mares Sun Briar had bred the previous year, seven foaled this spring. With Sun Briar's breeding career underway, Kilmer now had time for his runners.

As perplexing a man as he was, Willis Sharpe Kilmer did bring a singular vitality and energy to racing. When Exterminator set a new Jamaica record of 1:51 1/5 for nine furlongs in the June 19 Long Beach Handicap, some say Kilmer took on a new obsession — for Exterminator to meet Man o' War. Others say

Kilmer went in the other direction — trying to assure the two horses did not meet. The summer and fall campaign of 1920 remains to this day a matter of perspective, depending on which camp one is in: Exterminator's or Man o' War's.

The first inkling they could meet was when Walter Vosburgh posted the weights for the Brooklyn Handicap at Aqueduct. Sir Barton topped the list with 128 pounds, with 119 for Exterminator, and 118 pounds to Man o' War, which was about five pounds over scale.

Man o' War had been eligible for months, but his connections didn't enter him. Guy Bedwell didn't have Sir Barton ready. And Exterminator, the only one to run, hadn't found his stride yet. He finished behind Cirrus, Boniface, and Mad Hatter. Exterminator then won two straight at Aqueduct, setting a track record of 1:44 in the mile and one-sixteenth Luke Blackburn Handicap on June 29, and four days later, beating Cirrus on a muddy track in the nine-furlong Brookdale Handicap. "When Exterminator feels right he is a horse of horses," an admiring journalist wrote in the *New York Herald*. "What we like most about Exterminator is the fact that he is...a two-miler — a stayer after the old cup horse type which is becoming extinct."

In the meantime Man o' War won the mile Stuyvesant Handicap for three-year-olds at Jamaica by eight lengths under 135 pounds, then ran into a buzz saw in the Dwyer Stakes at Aqueduct on July 10. John P. Grier grabbed hold of him soon after the start and didn't want to let go. He even sent the crowd into cardiac arrest when he briefly forged to the front. But Man o' War prevailed and posted a new American record for nine furlongs in 1:49 1/5.

In late July trains with horse-laden boxcars headed for the Spa. Exterminator took a little detour into Canada for the $10,000-added Frontier Handicap at Windsor on July 14. He only managed to earn third money of one-thousand dollars. Then it was on to Saratoga for the mile and a quarter Saratoga Handicap on opening day. In addition to Exterminator, the field was solid gold: Mad Hatter, The Porter, Wildair, and Sir Barton. The track was fast.

Sir Barton, who bore high weight of 129 pounds, hadn't raced since winning the Rennert Handicap on May 4, but his recent trials were impressive, "and a majority of the horsemen say that the horse which beats him will take the major portion of the purse." Exterminator, with 126 pounds and Andy Schuttinger up, was nearing peak form but wasn't quite there yet; and Sam Hildreth's pair, Mad Hatter and Cirrus, "are on edge for a startling performance and promises to run a record breaking race." [1]

It had been hoped Man o' War would run, but Sir Barton made up for Big Red's absence. With Earl Sande up, he turned back one challenger after another. The Porter tried first. Then, it was Mad Hatter's turn, and as he ranged up alongside the leader, his jockey, Buddy Ensor, shouted to Sande, "I've gotcha boy!" Sande just smiled and let out an inch or so of rein and left Mad Hatter struggling. Exterminator moved to within three-quarters of a length with a quarter-mile left, and Sande hit Sir Barton twice. "He pulls away," Sande recalled, "and we coast under the wire three lengths' winner..." in 2:01 4/5, a new track record. [2]

The clamor for a three-way meeting had begun back in late spring and with Sir Barton's sterling performance and Man o' War's triumph in the Miller Stakes under 131 pounds five days later, the level neared fever pitch. Exterminator lost some backing briefly when he went under to Gnome, giving him nineteen pounds, in the Champlain Handicap on August 14. But what followed was a metamorphosis, and Exterminator emerged a lion.

Exterminator traveled to Windsor again, first for the $10,000-added Windsor Jockey Club Handicap. No soft spot here, not with the likes of Boniface, who was enjoying one of the best seasons in his distinguished career, and Wildair, and Slippery Elm. Exterminator, getting five pounds from Boniface, overtook Wildair in the stretch and ran the final furlong in :12 2/5 on the way to equaling Windsor's nine-furlong mark of 1:51 1/5. Boniface was far back in third. Exterminator ended his latest sortie north by winning the George Hendrie Memorial Handicap under 131 pounds in near track-record time for a mile and one-sixteenth, this while eased up. He was now primed for a late-season run at the championship. To win, he'd have to catch Sir Barton.

To recount the year without the Triple Crown winner would be akin to trying to draw a triangle using two lines. Sir Barton was a bantam next to his rivals. He stood about 15.3 hands and weighed 900 pounds, 950 tops. But he was described as a "bull of a horse...a glutton for work." The colt had his Achilles heel, however. He had shelly, brittle hooves. Hard surfaces were murder.

Exterminator returned to Saratoga, his purse fatter by nearly fifteen thousand dollars from his Canadian jaunt. Sir Barton had also gone across the border, winning the Dominion Handicap at Fort Erie on August 11 with 134 pounds. And ten days after that, Man o' War equaled Saratoga's track record of 2:01 4/5 for ten furlongs in winning the Travers Stakes. All three were among the entries for the Saratoga Cup on Tuesday, August 31.

"That [Guy] Bedwell will have him [Sir Barton] on edge for the cup is a foregoine [sic] conclusion," a writer for *The Sun and New York Herald* penned on August 8. "That he will start him also is certain, as he has always raced his horses when they were ready, and has never shown a disposition to dodge the issue with any rivals."

The race of the century was still on as late as the 26th. But two days later, Man o' War was instead shipped to Belmont Park for the September 4 Lawrence Realization Stakes, a race for which he was already scheduled.

That same day, Sir Barton, carrying 133 pounds, bested Gnome after a hard-fought contest in the Merchants' and Citizens' Handicap, casting doubts that even a bull of a horse could come back against Exterminator in three days. A journalist writing for *The Sun and New York Herald* under the name "Daniel" didn't like it a bit. As far as he was concerned, the one-time "Race of the Century" now loomed as nothing more than a rerun of the Saratoga Handicap.

"It is to be deplored that Sir Barton will not meet Man o' War in the Saratoga Cup. The supposition had been that if Sir Barton did well in the Merchants' and Citizens' Handicap the race with the Riddle star would be a certainty. However, Mr. Riddle has withdrawn his colt. His friends say that he tired of the battledore and shuttlecock tactics of Commander Ross. No matter what the reason the fact remains that the race of the year has been wiped off the programme...It looks as if the owners of Sir Barton and Man o' War are afraid of each other and do not care to risk a meeting."

On Monday the traditional late-August thunderstorms bore down on Saratoga Springs from the Adirondacks, and Sir Barton withdrew from

Tuesday's cup. Interest plummeted.

To think that the Saratoga Cup was any less a race than it was a month ago riled the Exterminator camp to no end. Healy had the gelding on his toes. Exterminator's eyes were bright. His coat glowed like polished brass. He was all "bone and muscle," wrote one admirer, "the tendons standing out like catgut." And under his agnomen, "Salvator," John Hervey described him as "Herculean..."

With the muddy track, no one cared to take on the bear except for W.R. Coe, who entered his three-year-old filly Cleopatra. But lest anyone think she was a patsy, the daughter of Corcyra had already proven she could hold her own against the boys. She had just finished conceding actual weight to males in the Huron Handicap and whipped them in American record time of 1:56 for a mile and three-sixteenths. She later would give the boys scale weight and a beating in the mile and three-quarters Latonia Championship.

But Healy had his gelding so ready that the pre-race instructions to jockey Charlie "Butts" Fairbrother oozed confidence. "Let this fellow run all the way and there won't be a contest. He'll run this mare dizzy in the first mile and you'll come home by yourself."

Charlie followed instructions to a tee. On a track described as heavy and greasy, Exterminator took the lead during the first quarter, ran on his own wits throughout, and won by six lengths in 2:56 2/5, a new American record for fourteen furlongs. "Exterminator showed by his race that even a Sir Barton or a Man o' War must do his best to beat him over a distance of ground," Henry King wrote in *The Sun and New York Herald*. "He covered the distance without doing his best at any stage of the journey...At the end he was only galloping..."

"Daniel" was still mad as a hornet:

"The Saratoga Cup, an old-fashioned race at an old-fashioned distance — looked like a race of a decade only a few days ago when there was a chance that it would bring together Sir Barton and Man o' War. But yesterday it degenerated into a match in which the result never was left in doubt. It was hardly fair to Cleopatra to send her against Exterminator. And it was hardly fair to the Saratoga Cup and the traditions of the event to make it a match in which only one horse had a chance."

It's difficult to conceive of a more one-sided event than Man o' War made the Lawrence Realization on September 4. At the end of the mile and five-eighths, the margin back to Hoodwink, his single opponent, could only be estimated at a hundred lengths, and he obliterated the old American standard.

Big Red's dominance only seemed to anger Willis Kilmer all the more. According to David Alexander, Kilmer became obsessed and "followed Riddle from track to track and club to club, shaking fifty thousand dollars in his face and demanding he put up the same stake for a race between Man o' War and Exterminator at weight-for-age. Riddle always smiled and suggested the two could meet in the normal course of their engagements..."

"We might have had a real test between two of the greatest," Alexander continued, "had Old Boiling Point...been successful in his attempts to match Exterminator against Man o' War in 1920." Alexander firmly believed that Riddle avoided Exterminator.

Not everyone agrees. In extensive research for a book on Man o' War, Dorothy Ours, education assistant at the National Museum of Racing and Hall of Fame in

Saratoga Springs, said she found nothing to suggest that Kilmer "pursued Sam Riddle from track to track."

Hopes for a dream race continued. Among the many tracks vying to bring the triumvirate together was Kenilworth Park in Windsor, Ontario. And the track's management hit the jackpot, two-thirds of it anyway. A.M. Orpen, the track's manager, offered a $75,000 winner-take-all purse plus a $5,000 gold cup. The race would be the Kenilworth Park Gold Cup, scheduled for mid-October, the distance a mile and a quarter at weight-for-age. Messrs. Riddle and Ross accepted their invitations and a piece in *The New York Times* on September 22 confirmed Kilmer's acceptance as well.

Then Kilmer put a fly in the ointment. He insisted the distance be a mile and a half and run under handicap conditions. Man o' War's connections said the distance was fine, but they would not allow Big Red to run at the mercy of a handicapper. So Exterminator was a no-show.

The race itself proved little. Taking nothing from Man o' War's performance, Sir Barton was badly compromised on Kenilworth's hard surface, and he was beaten seven lengths in a track-record time of 2:03. He didn't win again in three starts and was retired. Matt Winn tried desperately to stage a race, but then Man o' War was retired.

Exterminator, however, was far from finished.

Years later, the author of a piece in *The Thoroughbred Record* reminisced about the two champions:

"During the war I saw a picture of stooped and knobby-wristed Vinegar Joe Stillwell standing alongside that pouter pigeon with peacock plumage, Georgie Patton. Old Joe wore rumpled fatigues and a long-outdated campaign hat...Patton, as usual, was an arrogant, burnished, breathing glass of military fashion...The two commanders bore little resemblance to each other except that each was among the greatest military leaders of his time. The photograph made me think of Exterminator and Man o' War."

Ironic that the image of two great military leaders reminded the writer of two horses with names intended for battle.

CHAPTER 9

"...gasping like a goldfish out of water"

J. Simon Healy was subdued as he saddled Exterminator for the Autumn Gold Cup on September 15. It was fifteen days since the gelding ran off with the Saratoga Cup; seven since Healy announced his resignation from the Kilmer barn. Tomorrow he would take over the stable of Cuban horseman A.H. Diaz. Today he was sending Exterminator out once more. He was looking forward to changing employers, but he hated losing Exterminator.

Fall hadn't begun, but the mornings had the feel of change. It wouldn't be long before the old oak and chestnut trees shading Belmont Park's saddling paddock, which Walter Vosburgh described as "the most beautiful seen anywhere," would shed their glorious plumage.

Opened in 1905, Belmont was a youngster compared with the elegant senior ladies of Lexington, Saratoga, and Pimlico. But the youngster had to survive a number of reversals over the next fifteen years. The reform blackout suspended racing from 1911 through 1912; fire in April of 1917 destroyed the grandstand and jockeys' quarters. Yet the spring meeting opened on time seven weeks later on Memorial Day. Following additional remodeling that stretched the grandstand to 950 feet, Belmont Park was the biggest racing plant in the United States in 1920 and, at a mile and a half, the longest.

Healy's instructions to Charlie Fairbrother were simple: "Lay off the pace until half a mile from home. He'll get you there." Exterminator had a lot of campaigning ahead of him. His schedule would unglue an ordinary horse — three more cup races after this one and the Bowie Handicap. Healy couldn't recall a horse ever winning five cups in one season, much less four in a row. Healy's successor, Will McDaniel, Henry's brother, had his work cut out for him.

Rumors circulated all week that Exterminator wasn't in shape, that he might not start. But the gelding was fine and would give his all that afternoon. He always did. The crowd was disappointed though when Mad Hatter was scratched. These two usually meant fireworks when they tangled. The fans did get their show, a "rattling good race," wrote Henry King in *The Sun and New York Herald* that "brought the crowd to its feet yelling like so many Comanche Indians."

Only Damask and Cleopatra, enjoying weight concessions of thirty and twenty-three pounds, respectively, challenged Exterminator, who was three pounds over scale with 128. Cleopatra led for a mile and a half before giving way to three-year-old Damask. At about this point, Fairbrother loosened the wraps and Exterminator started to roll. The crowd groaned when he got pinched on the rail momentarily, but Fairbrother swung him to the outside and set sail for Damask; "...it was hammer and tongs from that point to the finish." [1]

Exterminator won with a last-second lunge, getting the two miles in 3:21 4/5, another American record. Henry King's admiration for him knew no bounds. The race was "remarkable and stamped him as the greatest cup horse in the country. He...won fighting as only a stout hearted thoroughbred can fight."

In the winner's circle, on the lawn in front of the

clubhouse, the congratulations and the praises flowed freely. Fighting tearing eyes, Healy smiled. But, as King continued, "...he was not jubilant, he was dejected. He was elated over the victory, but he was parting with the thoroughbred he loved...Exterminator was his pet...attached to him as a man would to a faithful dog."

Ten days after coming to the Kilmer barn, Will McDaniel sent Exterminator out to win the ten-furlong Toronto Autumn Cup at Woodbine. Under top weight of 132 pounds, Exterminator stepped the final quarter in :24 3/5 and edged the good three-year-old filly My Dear (getting forty pounds) by a head. His time of 2:04 2/5 was only a tick off the track standard.

Seven days later Exterminator added the Ontario Jockey Club Cup at two and a quarter-miles to his collection. Running under wraps on a heavy track, Exterminator packed his 134-pound impost with ease to prevail by a length and a quarter. Then it was on to Pimlico, where he would end this season as he had the last, in the Bowie Handicap and Pimlico Cup.

The Bowie at a mile and a half attracted a stellar field, including Mad Hatter and Boniface to whom Exterminator, with 135 pounds, spotted fifteen and thirteen pounds, respectively. The big gelding found himself trapped on the rail and could do no better than fifth once he was free, with Mad Hatter nosing out Boniface in near-record time.

The 1920 Pimlico Cup carried a purse doubled from the previous year's $5,000-added and lured several of the Bowie starters, including Mad Hatter and Boniface. Under top weight of 126 pounds, Exterminator, kept under a tight hold by jockey Buddy Ensor, had enough early speed to keep himself out of trouble. After a mile and a quarter, Ensor let him go. He reached Mad Hatter, but that one had nothing left. Exterminator appeared to be on his way to an uncontested victory when Ensor heard the crowd roar. He glanced back to see Boniface coming hard. Those two fought from mid-stretch on with Exterminator prevailing by a nose. His time of 3:53 obliterated twenty seconds from his own track standard in the inaugural running the year before, when the race was run in heavy going.

Exterminator had raised the bar to an unprecedented level with five cup victories, four in a row. He also garnered ten wins in seventeen starts and six track or American records from a mile and one-sixteenth to

two and a quarter miles. Not so long ago, Sir Barton had been conceded the older horse championship, but at year's end it was Exterminator, with earnings of $52,805.

With Man o' War gone from the scene, Exterminator had become the new Caesar.

In 1921 writer Bill Vreeland gave Exterminator the official nickname Old Bones, which had belonged to another beloved gelding from years ago named Raceland. That same year Henry McDaniel went to work for Commander Ross.

Ross had the most successful and fastest-growing stable in racing and had topped the earnings list in 1918 and 1919. Such was his stable of outstanding gallopers that his son J.K.M. Ross referred to them as "heavy artillery." The man who put the Ross barn on top, trainer Guy Bedwell, was retiring, and McDaniel was hired to replace him. Since leaving Kilmer at the end of 1919, McDaniel had handled Robert Gerry's stable with noted success, but the opportunity to saddle a Boniface was hard to ignore, even though the trainer knew that at some point his horses would have to compete against Exterminator. On April 30

McDaniel sent Boniface out to win the Philadelphia Handicap.

Under the handling of three different trainers in his first nine starts, Exterminator was slow getting on track in 1921, beginning with two second-place finishes for Will McDaniel, to Mad Hatter in the Kings County Handicap on May 7 and to Blazes a week later in the Excelsior Handicap.

The Long Beach Handicap on May 21 was a typical Exterminator/Mad Hatter performance. Sharing top weight of 130 pounds, these titans ran one-two from the rise of the barrier, with Mad Hatter setting a lively pace: a half-mile in :48, six furlongs in 1:12 2/5.

Jamaica was an exaggerated egg-shaped course, and in the sweeping far turn, the large end of the "egg," Exterminator put a head in front and stayed there. His time of 1:50 for the nine furlongs cut one and three-fifths seconds from his record set in the previous year's renewal.

In two more starts for McDaniel, Exterminator was fifth in the Suburban Handicap on June 4 under 133 pounds and third in the Brooklyn Handicap, won by the three-year-old sensation Grey Lag. In ill health for

some time, Will McDaniel retired. He died in 1923.

F. Curtis trained Exterminator for three races, with the gelding winning the twelve-furlong Independence Handicap on July 4, coming just three ticks within the track mark, and finishing third in both the Daniel Boone and Frontier handicaps on July 9 and July 12, respectively. Curtis' quick exit may have had something to do with the arrival of a familiar face, with a new trainer's license in his pocket.

Bill Knapp had been Kilmer's contract rider in the early years; he brought Exterminator home in the Derby and was the only rider to win with Sun Briar. He had had a distinguished career, for which he was later inducted into the Racing Hall of Fame in 1969. But, grounded by weight, Knapp turned to training.

Bill, or Willie as some called him, Knapp trained Exterminator the rest of 1921, winning six of eight, the first a hard-fought victory over Mad Hatter in the Merchants' and Citizens' Handicap on August 27. The victory was a special one for Knapp. In one of those little bits of racing lore, "Big Bill" was aboard when Exterminator won his first stakes, the Kentucky Derby. Now, Exterminator provided the first stakes win for trainer Knapp.

August 31 dawned rainy in Saratoga Springs, and for the third straight year, the Saratoga Cup was run on a muddy track. In forty previous renewals, the Cup had been won back to back only five times, including Exterminator's. And there had never been a walkover. But when the rains came, no one wanted any part of Exterminator. Knapp's instructions to Bill Kelsay beforehand were to the point: "No heroics. Just a good gallop." And that was the way of the 1921 Saratoga Cup.

The mile and three-quarters gallop was a great prep for the Autumn Gold Cup at Belmont Park on September 16. Bellsolar, Exterminator's only rival, wasn't a bad racehorse; Exterminator just made him look that way, beating him by six lengths in what was little more than a two-mile workout. Knapp then put the Kilmer gelding on a northbound train for the Toronto Autumn Cup on September 24 and a meeting with the Henry McDaniel-trained Boniface, probably the biggest gun in the Ross arsenal.

Boniface would rank in the top four among the year's older horses, with all but one of his eight victories coming in stakes. For the Toronto Autumn Cup, he was getting nine pounds from his rival, who had been slapped with 137 pounds. Another crack runner was the four-year-old mare My Dear, whose seven victories in 1921 included the Hamilton Cup, the Toronto Cup Handicap, and the National Handicap over males.

Like Mad Hatter, Boniface usually ran Exterminator right to the wire but this time lacked his usual punch and finished fifth. It was My Dear, benefiting from a twenty-pound weight concession, who provided the fireworks and forced Exterminator to within a second of the track record for ten furlongs, clocked in 2:05 1/5.

Exterminator's streak ended on October 8 with a third-place finish under 135 pounds in the mile and a half Annapolis Handicap. The first two finishers, The Porter and My Dear, were in receipt of a combined thirty-six pounds. Following a bit of a breather, Exterminator beat My Dear in a ten-furlong overnight handicap at Laurel. But the campaign, especially the successive starts with weights ranging from 132 to 137 pounds, was taking its toll. When a pair of ordinary three-year-olds beat him in the Lexington Cup, many thought he should be shelved for the year. But the year couldn't end without his running in the Pimlico Cup.

Only two rivals challenged him in the mud: Boniface and four-year-old Lady Emmeline. The filly was outclassed before even taking to the course, but Boniface was coming in off a near-record win in the Bowie Handicap and was as sharp as Henry McDaniel could make him. He was also getting five pounds. Those who had witnessed the previous year's block-buster might have thought they were watching a rerun. Except the sequel was much better.

The start for the eighteen-furlong race came in the backstretch and so part of the early going was obstruct-ed by Pimlico's "mountain." Exterminator, carrying Albert Johnson and 126 pounds, was quickest off the blocks from his rail position. Johnson very quickly put a hold on the power under him. Still they had a length advantage on Boniface coming into the front straight the first time. Exterminator's fractions reflected his control of the pace in the mud: :55 at the end of the first half-mile and 1:51 at the mile. Into the backstretch for the final lap, they disappeared briefly behind the hill. When they re-emerged, Boniface had closed to

within a head. Earl Sande gave his mount rein and Boniface's stride lengthened. Exterminator and Boniface swept around the far turn and into the top of the stretch as closely matched as a harnessed team, first one head bobbing in front and then the other.

"It was as great a race as any one ever saw over a distance of ground," began the coverage in *The Thoroughbred Record*, "for there never was a time from start to finish of the long journey of two miles and a quarter that Exterminator and Boniface were more than a length apart. At times they were racing nose and nose, and over on the backstretch when they made their final lap they were so close together that many of those watching the race from the ground could only see the one horse."

At the same time Sande asked Boniface for his move, Johnson merely loosened his hold and Exterminator quickened his pace, with the seventh quarter in :25 3/5. Years later, Albert Johnson recalled, "Exterminator needed no jockey. He was the most intelligent horse I ever rode. He made his own pace, moving when it was time...Sande let out the wraps a little on Boniface, and I felt Old Bones lengthen his stride to match the spurt. Turning for home, Boniface was asked for his best, and he gave it like the good horse he was. But I didn't have to call on Exterminator. That old fellow knew what was needed and willingly offered his best to cling to his narrow head lead." [2]

They turned into the stretch for the last time locked in combat, neither willing to separate. Johnson continued, "Sande was working like a wild man on Boniface as we hit the sixteenth pole, plying whip, hands and heels. Somehow I hadn't the slightest worry, for Old Bones just kept plugging along — always holding his small winning edge. And in just that way, we hit the line." [3]

The capacity-plus crowd made a sound likely not heard since Joshua brought down the walls of Jericho. There was glory enough for both, and a breathless Henry McDaniel received as many congratulations as Bill Knapp. One journalist asked McDaniel what he thought about Boniface coming so close only to lose. McDaniel gasped, "Didn't you see? Exterminator pulled a knife on him!"

Some criticized Exterminator's close finishes. But

Knapp found them exhilarating. "He willed it so," he said years later, "leaving everyone, including myself, gasping like a goldfish out of water." [4]

EXTERMINATOR

CHAPTER 10

"the last great campaign"

The saga of Kilmer's revolving door continued with Eugene Wayland, Exterminator's seventh trainer, as the 1922 campaign began.

When Kilmer split his growing stable into two divisions at the end of 1921, Bill Knapp assumed he would continue training Exterminator. But Kilmer wouldn't say one way or the other, so Knapp quit.

Gene Wayland had been training for the successful W.J. Salmon stable, and surely he weighed the opportunity to handle Exterminator against the uncertainties of Willis Kilmer and decided it was worth a go.

At seven Exterminator was at the top of his game. By April 15 Wayland had him stripped for speed to take on Billy Kelly at equal weights of 132 pounds in the six-furlong Harford Handicap. Not only was Commander Ross' six-year-old gelding the era's top sprinter, but Billy

Kelly could stretch his speed to win the ten-furlong Connaught Cup with 135 pounds and beat no less than Mad Hatter at nine furlongs. On paper, he had the edge: six furlongs was his distance, the Harford his race, having won it the past three years. Exterminator hadn't competed at less than a mile for three years. Billy Kelly went off as the near-even-money favorite.

Despite the supporting evidence favoring Billy Kelly, Exterminator won going away on a muddy track.

Billy Kelly "went wrong" afterward and was retired for the year, but Ross still had Boniface, and McDaniel put that horse in the Philadelphia Handicap field, which included Exterminator, on April 22. Cut off at the three-eighths pole by another horse, Exterminator still came back to run Boniface to a nose.

The mile and one-sixteenth Pimlico Spring Handicap on May 6 was typical of the history between these two. Exterminator, under 133 pounds, had a neck advantage in the stretch, but Boniface, with 125, shoved his head in front with a sixteenth remaining. Refusing to concede, Exterminator found another gear and snatched the victory in the last half stride. His time, 1:45 4/5, was only three ticks off the track mark. It was the opening salvo of a most remarkable run over the next six weeks.

Exterminator won both starts at Churchill Downs —
the nine-furlong Clark Handicap on May 20, with 133
pounds, and the ten-furlong Kentucky Handicap seven
days later with a crushing 138. Then, in a span of just
eleven days in June, he captured three races in New
York: at Belmont Park, the nine-furlong Bayside
Handicap on June 5 with 133 pounds against Be
Frank's 107; and on June 13 the mile and one-sixteenth Garden City Handicap under 135 pounds, conceding seven to Mad Hatter; then at Aqueduct, on June
16, what most historians agree was the greatest race of
Exterminator's career.

He went into the June 16 Brooklyn Handicap lug-
ging 135 pounds for the second time in three days.
Rancocas Stable's Grey Lag, the previous year's three-
year-old champion, was backed down to 4-5.
Exterminator with two unsuccessful attempts in this
race, including the 1921 running to Grey Lag, closed at
3-2. Three other starters were badly outclassed.

Races of nine furlongs over the old Aqueduct mile
and a quarter course started from a chute on the backstretch and presented a straight run of nearly half a

mile to the far turn. In the Brooklyn, pacesetter Polly Ann was cooked after stepping the distance in :47 3/5. Going into the turn, she drifted out, and Exterminator slipped through on the rail. Jockey Laverne Fator also gunned Grey Lag through and maneuvered the chestnut son of Star Shoot so close to Exterminator that Albert Johnson couldn't use his whip. The pair turned the corner into the stretch together.

In *At the Wire: Horse Racing's Greatest Moments*, Edward L. Bowen quoted a *Thoroughbred Record* reporter's description of the finish: "In a stretch duel that will be long memorable to racegoers, the ever youthful Exterminator — greatest gelding of them all — shouldering 135 pounds like a Titan, wore down the lighter weighted Grey Lag and outgamed him in the final furlongs…" Exterminator refused to let go and, "though he threw his tail in the air once, as though indicating that he was giving up his last ounce, he never faltered…old Exterminator had finally earned a lead of a head, and it was his to hold."

Trainer Sam Hildreth acknowledged Exterminator's victory, but attributed Grey Lag's defeat to Exterminator's shorter inside trip. "This is fallacious,"

Neil Newman recalled years later. "...Fator had Johnson so pinned in that Exterminator's rider could not use his whip. Another point — I never recall a race in which Exterminator got his head in front in the stretch that he was beaten to the wire."

But all wasn't well afterwards. Exterminator was blowing harder than usual. And that tail flicking during the drive...Wayland wondered had they stretched the old fellow too far? He watched the gelding for any lameness. He was looking in the wrong place.

"He was never the same thereafter," wrote Newman, who accompanied Wayland to the barn later that afternoon. Always the tiger at his feed box, Exterminator was standing quietly in his stall, his feed untouched. Even the spark seemed to be gone.

"How is he, Blink?" Wayland asked Blink McClosky, his barn's foreman.

"He turned his tail to the feed box and won't eat. He never done that before. Boss, he looks like he's all through."

Meanwhile, Willis Kilmer's breeding operation had outgrown Sun Briar Court, and he looked around for land, preferably in Virginia. His agent came back with the description of some available acreage near New Market in the Shenandoah Valley. Here Willis Kilmer built Court Manor, which would become the breeding center of the Old Dominion, ruled by Sun Briar.

Following the Brooklyn, Wayland suggested putting Exterminator back for a while rather than run him again less than three weeks later in the mile and a half Independence Handicap under 140 pounds. But the $15,450 winner's purse, Kilmer argued, would put Exterminator within $22,000 or so of Man o' War's record $249,465. Not surprisingly, it was too much. Exterminator "appeared in distress at the end of the first mile," the race chart commented. [1] Albert Johnson said he just "folded up after a mile."

Joe Estes, the editor of *The Blood-Horse*, was so upset that he composed what he called "a silly little ditty":

"There was a camel, whose back was broke,
One sprig of straw made the poor beast croak.
It's a dang good thing, for them that gamble,
Exterminator ain't no camel."

Kilmer said nothing. But when he was rebuked for running Exterminator back in the Saratoga Handicap on August 1, with the gelding finishing last with 137 pounds to Grey Lag's 130, he fired back insisting "the horse was fit and well, he had earned his weight and one never got weight off by staying in the barn and start he would. And start he did, but he ran badly and finished fifth..." [2]

In the week leading up to the Saratoga Cup on August 31, rumors abounded that Exterminator wouldn't attempt a fourth win. He did, and led every step of the fourteen furlongs to beat Mad Hatter by a neck. "Both Johnson and Sande rode like jehus," Newman wrote, "but Exterminator's heart supplemented Johnson's head..." [3] His fans began calling for his retirement. What else did he have to prove? What could top four Saratoga Cups?

Well, three Toronto Autumn Cups. Three Pimlico Cups. Not to mention the deficit he still needed to overtake Man o' War. He narrowed the gap with the $12,800 purse for winning his third Toronto Autumn Cup on September 20, carrying 132 pounds.

It was about this time that Kilmer received an invitation from Thomas Carey to bring Exterminator to Hawthorne in Cicero, Illinois. Built in 1891 by the stormy Ed Corrigan, Hawthorne was attempting to reopen following a checkered hiatus. It, and the older

Washington Park in Chicago, had been closed during the racing blackout. Washington Park was dismantled. Hawthorne fell into disrepair and was sold to the Carey family for only two-thousand dollars when Corrigan went bankrupt.

Tom Carey held a three-day meeting in 1914 to test the local waters and, in 1916, opened for thirteen days. For a main attraction he "borrowed" from his defunct neighbor the popular American Derby. Three-year-old Dodge won in track-record time of 2:04 3/5. Six years later, determined to bring racing back to Illinois, Carey needed a big attraction — the most popular horse in America. Would Kilmer be interested in starting Exterminator in a special race against Dodge's track record? Carey promised no remuneration for Exterminator's appearance.

Considering Exterminator's staggering campaign, most owners would have said no thanks. Kilmer said yes.

Some twenty-five thousand fans converged upon Hawthorne that September 30, a steamy Saturday. "They came by train, elevated, surface cars, and countless automobiles and taxis of all descriptions. The roads overflowed for a mile approaching the track." When

Exterminator stepped on the course, the "tremendous crowd simply went wild at the mere sight of this famous racer..." [4]

The event was given a half-number by the *Daily Racing Form* and listed as the fifth race on a seven-race card, no conditions or purse indicated. In correspondence with this writer, the late Amelia K. Buckley, librarian with the Keeneland Library, wrote that Exterminator's presence was merely a "drawing card."

Unsure about the bottom of a track so recently covered in weeds, Gene Wayland had no intentions of letting Exterminator go full out. He told Johnson to hold him for a mile then "let him run the final quarter on his own." So under a snug hold, he posted a lazy mile in 1:45 1/5 and, when given his head, stepped the final quarter in :24 4/5. His final time of 2:10 was far off the mark, but the racing chart noted that he "ran as good a race as could be expected on a new and slow track." [5]

Today, the event is recorded as an official start and an unplaced finish against Exterminator's record, but such was not always the case. John Hervey, the noted historian of the early twentieth century, flatly stated it was a "certain courtesy accorded to him to which *under*

a strict interpretation of the rules he was not entitled."

Information in the 1936 *American Racing Manual* shows Exterminator's 1922 record as seventeen starts and ten wins, but only four unplaced finishes (the exhibition being counted as a fifth unplaced effort by some accounts). [For more on revising Exterminator's record, see Postscript.]

Exterminator's season was far from over. He raced three times at Laurel within two weeks, top-weighted with either 132 or 133 pounds each time. He won the $10,000-added Laurel Stakes at a mile and finished fourth in the Arundel and Washington handicaps. It was through no fault of his that Exterminator didn't win a fourth Pimlico Cup on November 11.

"Exterminator tired after forcing an unduly fast pace for the first mile and finished an eased up third."[6] But the race chart told only half the story of his career-worst finish in the race.

With Albert Johnson hospitalized with appendicitis, Benny Marinelli was given the ride. Wayland's instructions were the same as they had been for months — save him as long as possible and let him win on his own courage. It should have been enough, for none of the four challengers could have made him break a sweat in the old days. Paul Jones was well past the form that won him a Derby. Captain Alcock was probably the best of the lot, winner of the Suburban, Brookdale, and Bowie handicaps, and Exterminator was giving him twenty pounds.

The race was lost when Exodus shot to the front after the break and Marinelli sent Exterminator after him. With Exodus reeling off quarters in the twenty-fours, including :24 flat for the third, Exterminator raced just a head behind until Exodus bolted to the outside fence with a mile to go and put Old Bones in the lead. Not surprisingly, Marinelli found an empty gas tank in the stretch, but to his credit the rider didn't go on with him. Exterminator, eased to a canter, finished third, thirty-one and a half lengths behind the winner, Captain Alcock.

Henry McDaniel, watching as a spectator, shook his head. A "bungling ride," he said afterward. [7]

"...badly ridden," wrote "Argus," in *The Thoroughbred Record*, "...the artistry of [Linus] McAtee on Capt. Alcock was far too much for Marinelli; had the jockeys been reversed, the old horse would have prevailed."

Exterminator would return in 1923. But as far as John Hervey was concerned, 1922 was Exterminator's "last great campaign...we may well pause here to sum up one of the most extraordinary thoroughbreds that has ever appeared and one whose like, very possibly, we shall not see again."

Most historians point to 1922 as the gelding's best year. His steadiness under staggering weights was incredible. In winning ten of his sixteen actual starts, he carried 130 pounds or more in nine, several at ten furlongs or longer. *The Thoroughbred Record*'s Charles Griffen Herring thought the defining moment came with Exterminator's fourth Saratoga Cup. The writer witnessed it, and while visiting Sun Briar Court a few days later, he stopped at Exterminator's empty stall and stood for the longest time, as though paying homage.

"...I felt again the tightening of the heart and moisture about my eyes as when I rose to my feet with the rest of the great concourse...and cheered him home in his heroic win for the fourth time of the Saratoga Cup. Everyone loves and reverences this brave and honest creature, and he will be remembered as long as generous hearts warm to brave and noble deeds."

EXTERMINATOR

CHAPTER 11

"An Exterminator story is always a good story"

S omeone suggested that of the nine different trainers who handled Exterminator, Eugene Wayland was the best. That he kept the gelding going following the Brooklyn and Independence handicaps to win a fourth Saratoga and third Toronto Autumn cups was a masterful job. But even his special touch likely wouldn't have helped in 1923.

Exterminator was eight. The campaigns were telling on him. But Willis Kilmer's goal was Man o' War's earnings record. Exterminator only needed some six-thousand dollars and change. All he had to do was remain sound, and if anyone could keep him on the track, it was Wayland. But Gene died on March 9 of a heart attack. Now it was up to the gelding's eighth trainer, forty-six-year-old Toronto native and former jockey William Shields, who would handle

Exterminator for his 1923 racing season. All twelve days of it.

The campaign kicked off with the Harford Handicap on April 16. After a slow start, Exterminator, ridden by Earl Sande, closed fast to finish third, a neck and a length out of first. The effort set him up perfectly for the Philadelphia Handicap five days later, and he looked so good in the paddock that the fans bet him down to less than even. Jockey Linus "Pony" McAtee saved him to the stretch where he let him go and he outlasted Paul Jones.

The win ensured a three-pound weight gain for the Old Dominion Handicap a week later. Swinging into the stretch turn, the light weight of the field, three-year-old Chickvale, took the lead from Paul Jones and drew clear. Exterminator raced into a forward position on the outside and was lapped on the leader turning into the stretch. With Albert Johnson back in the irons, Exterminator engaged in another shootout. He had the heart, but the thirty-one-pound weight difference took its toll and Chickvale prevailed by a nose.

Exterminator finished very lame, and rumors were passed along that he would never run again.

"He is not hopelessly broken down as the hysterical reports first sent out about his lameness held," *The Thoroughbred Record* reported a month later. "He will be racing again in the autumn, after a summer's rest at Mr. Kilmer's Remlik Hall in the tidewater of Virginia, and Kentucky racing patrons may see him galloping in another Latonia Cup...But that will be another good story. An Exterminator story is always a good story...Racing folk and persons who do not take a lively interest in the doings of thoroughbreds, but who know about Exterminator...want to see him go on until he fixes a world mark in earnings that will never be touched. And it is within the limits of possibility that he may do it."

Exterminator didn't race again that year. And Shields, who was said to be in bad health when he took over the Kilmer stable, died on September 1. "Will Shields was training Exterminator when [the] season opened; but Shields was living on borrowed time himself. He died before Saratoga, and was in no condition to look after Exterminator." [1]

Meanwhile, in a remarkable three-year-old campaign, the great Zev had supplanted both Man o' War

and Isinglass on the earnings list with just over $301,000. Had the bar been set out of Exterminator's reach for good?

One of the richest races in North America was the mile and a quarter Coffroth Handicap, run at an obscure mile track in Tijuana, Mexico, just south of the U.S. border and eighteen miles from San Diego. The track opened in January 1916 and the following year inaugurated the Coffroth Handicap, with Sasin earning four-thousand dollars for the win. In 1923 Henry McDaniel saddled Rebuke for Commander Ross for the winner's purse of $29,475. For the 1924 renewal, track owner Sunny Jim Coffroth promised a forty-percent purse hike.

Since Zev had thrown a monkey wrench into Kilmer's plans, Old Bones now needed more than $53,000. The Coffroth payoff would punch a big hole in the deficit.

Henry McDaniel was in Tijuana training the Ross stable when Kilmer contacted him with the possibility of training Exterminator. McDaniel must have given it careful thought. Kilmer had gone through a half dozen trainers since McDaniel quit in 1919. What writer Ned

Welch once called the "I Trained for Willis Sharpe Kilmer Club." [2] Still, Kilmer's enthusiasm for racing was contagious to everyone around him, and McDaniel agreed. After the longest rail journey of his life, Exterminator arrived in Mexico from the East Coast soon after the first of the year.

In a place described by David Alexander "as grotesque a setting as could possibly be conceived for the richest race the Sport of Kings had ever offered," Exterminator's senses were assailed by a myriad of strange sounds and smells. "A Mexican village," Alexander continued, "where peons slept beneath their sombreros on dusty streets and stray curs had the starved and humpbacked look of coyotes."

The track, said historian Tom Gilcoyne, was built partly in a dry wash and was destroyed when a storm came down out of the mountains and sent a flood down the wash. It didn't matter; another racing facility was already being built on the other end of town. Agua Caliente, an architectural gem and a splendid racetrack, opened on December 28, 1929. When the Coffroth became the Agua Caliente Handicap in 1930, it was the first to offer a $100,000 purse.

On February 17, 1924, Exterminator went to the starting line for a prep race at a mile and seventy yards. Under allowance conditions, he carried 113 pounds, getting three pounds from Supercargo and Dorius. He looked every bit a ready racehorse, and fans knocked him down to thirty cents on the dollar. The gelding galloped under Albert Johnson's firm hold for more than three-quarters of a mile, then swept effortlessly to the front and won by a length. The $490 winner's share was barely a teaspoon in a bucket of what Exterminator needed, but if he looked this good in the Coffroth with its $43,000-plus paycheck, then Zev's reign could be a short one.

It might have been the six weeks off between the prep and the Coffroth on March 30. But for whatever reason, Exterminator was terribly short.

He was high weight with 130 pounds and conceded from five to thirty-five pounds to seventeen rivals. The gelding went off coupled with Commander Ross' Muttikins as a McDaniel-trained entry that the fans backed at odds of $1.60-1. But it was Runstar who led from the start and held off Osprey by a nose at the wire. Exterminator had a good trip and was closing in the stretch, but he tired in the final furlong to finish fourth for a $1,250 check.

A day or so later Exterminator was back on the train and arrived in Maryland for Havre de Grace's meeting. In the Edgewood Handicap on April 17 and carrying just 107 pounds, he was hard-ridden by new jockey P. Walls to beat Golden Sphere by half a length at a mile and seventy yards.

Trouble brewed once again between Henry McDaniel and Willis Kilmer, this time over Exterminator. That the gelding was all out under 107 pounds spoke volumes about his condition. But just two days after the Edgewood, Exterminator started in the Philadelphia Handicap under top weight of 125 pounds and conceding up to twenty pounds to five rivals. Coupled as an entry with Ross' New Hampshire, the two went off as the crowd's favorite on the heavy track. No longer was he able to skip through the mud as lightly as a dragon-fly on a pond. Despite Albert Johnson's efforts to keep him off the rail and where the going was better, Exterminator floundered around and finished fifth, eight and a quarter lengths behind the winner, Spot Cash, who was that year's leading four-year-old.

McDaniel later referred to his second split with Kilmer as a "disagreement." But it was common knowledge that the trainer wanted to see Exterminator retired. "Exterminator is still sound," Kilmer argued. McDaniel quit rather than argue the fine point between soundness and wear and tear. For the final three races of his career, the gelding was turned over to John I. Smith.

Exterminator lacked early speed and finished third in the Merchants Handicap at Pimlico on May 1, his last start in the states. Old Bones ended his career in two starts north of the border. The first was at Blue Bonnets in Montreal on June 7, where the crowd leaned toward fellow Canadian J.K.L. Ross' four-year-old Golden Rule and made him favorite. But Exterminator, with Jimmie Wallace (jockey number eighteen) up, looked like the Exterminator of old. He won handily, and his time for the mile, 1:39 4/5, was just two seconds off the track record on a rain-slowed surface.

On June 21, he went to the post for the Queen's Hotel Handicap at Dorval Park, not far from Blue Bonnets. Spot Cash was back, having earned his top weight of 128 pounds with victories in the Pimlico

Spring Handicap and Windsor Hotel Cup Handicap.
The four-year-old son of Broomstick would finish the
season ranked among older horses ahead of Zev and
Mad Hatter. The fans made Old Bones the favorite;
maybe it had to do with its being his ninety-ninth trip
to the post in actual competition. He looked particularly alert during the running and laid just off Digit's
lively pace. After six furlongs, Spot Cash made his
move. Exterminator moved with him, and the three
matched strides.

The crowd rose to its feet with a loud cheer. Spot
Cash forged to the front with Digit hanging on stub-
bornly and Exterminator launching a move that would
put him right up front. The cheering grew louder as
Exterminator closed in on the leaders. Then just as
quickly, he faltered and faded to fourth. Wallace tried
to ease him, but Exterminator fought back. Winning
was out of the question. It had become a battle for dig-
nity, and Old Bones put forth one final surge to beat
Digit by a neck for third. Just beyond the wire,
Exterminator pulled up lame.

It was nothing serious, but he wouldn't race any
more in 1924. "There was some thought of racing him

at 10," Joe Hirsch wrote seventy years later, "but his retirement was announced at the end of the 1924 campaign...His earnings of $252,996 placed him second on the all-time list to Zev...and his fame, earned with honesty and perseverance, lasted through the end of the century." [3]

So passed "the last great cup horse of the American turf," Neil Newman wrote in *The Morning Telegraph* in 1933, "and it is questionable if we shall ever see Exterminator's equal.

"Exterminator was truly the 'last of the Romans.' "

EXTERMINATOR

CHAPTER 12

"...quite a journey's end"

Exterminator's mystique continued to grow after he retired. Aided by a ten hands-high pony.

By the first full year of his retirement, Old Bones missed the racetrack environment and had become so mopey that the Kilmers decided to get him a companion. Only he didn't give a whit for the usual mascots, dogs and cats, or goats. When he appeared to take an interest in the little Sicilian donkeys the Kilmers raised at Remlik Hall, the subject of Shetland ponies came up — they're more rugged than the donkeys. A couple of sources reported Exterminator had a Sicilian donkey named "Mussolini" as a companion, but then entered Peanuts I, the first of three.

Was there an earlier Peanuts, though? In their book on Man o' War, authors Page Cooper and Roger Treat wrote that when he was three, Man o' War "knew

Peanuts, Exterminator's pony mascot, and all the goats and cats and chickens that made the Eastern tracks."

Exterminator had been retired to Remlik Hall following his injury at Dorval Park. Some say he went to Sun Briar Court first, but reliable sources identify Remlik Hall, Kilmer's training facility down on the Rappahannock River in Virginia's tidewater country. His groom there was one Milford, or Milton, Bray.

Little has been written of Peanuts I. But when he died in the stall he shared with Exterminator, our gentle giant was turned into seventeen hands of anguished terror.

Bray described the scene. Exterminator "dug a hole in the stall (straw) as deep as this chair I'm sitting in and wouldn't let anyone in. It took three men to hold him while I got the pony out. He wouldn't eat and wouldn't come out of his stall. We tried putting goats and donkeys in with him, but he just had a fit. Finally, Mr. Kilmer brought another pony...I put him in the stall and Exterminator came at him with his mouth open as if to bite him. The pony gave him a good kick, and they were best of friends after that." [1]

Mike Terry was Exterminator's groom later on. He

153

was also the Kilmer stable's stud groom at Sun Briar Court and Court Manor, Kilmer's breeding facility near New Market, Virginia. Terry recalled that Peanuts II lived to be thirty-five and spent seventeen of those years with Exterminator. When the little fellow began to look like he could go any time, the Kilmers brought in another Shetland, named Teddy.

"One day," Terry recalled, " 'Slim' saw the new pony and chased him toward St. Patrick's Cemetery [about four-fifths of a mile west of Sun Briar Court]. He wouldn't have anything to do with the new horse 'til Peanuts II died. Then we renamed Teddy Peanuts III, and the two of them became the best of friends." [2]

Remlik Hall deserves a fair share of attention here, for it brought out more facets of the mercurial Willis Kilmer than his other estates. One even got the impression it was his favorite place.

He had begun purchasing land in Middlesex County in 1909, more in 1917. He changed the name of the place, Streets Post Office, to Remlik Hall and renovated a fifty-two-room antebellum mansion that perched on a point overlooking the Rappahannock River. Willis and Sarah Kilmer, his second wife whom he married in

1932, filled the house with rare art and antiques. It was here he hosted those dinners that often changed locations in mid-course. By the early 1930s, the training farm, well equipped with both indoor and outdoor tracks, was considered the finest in Virginia.

Its fifteen-hundred acres harbored a wide and diverse habitat, including two and a half miles of river frontage near where the Rappahannock joined Chesapeake Bay; stands of dense woods providing sanctuary for quail and other birds; and hundreds of acres planted with food grains and staples.

Exterminator was twenty-two when *The Blood-Horse* writer Humphrey S. Finney visited Remlik Hall late in December 1937, but he found "...plenty of fire in the old chap's eye yet and he carries his years exceptionally well. His hair is long but has the sheen of health, and his flesh is firm. Exterminator and his tiny paddock-mate are cared for by a leisurely Virginian called 'Pitchfork.' " Kilmer called Bray "Pitchfork" because he could never remember the groom's name.

"Kilmer loved his horses as much as most people love their children," Bray told Larry Chowning years later. He recalled a young filly that got loose one night and injured herself badly in some electric wires. When Bray advised putting her down, Kilmer wouldn't hear it. "No, she is my baby. I nursed her myself with a bottle." But the filly didn't survive her injuries. [3]

But Exterminator, despite all his accomplishments, "wasn't Mr. Kilmer's favorite horse. Anytime a thunderstorm come up, I was to bring in all the horses, but Mr. Kilmer would always tell me to put the other horses in before Exterminator." That isn't to say he was neglected.

"I was to keep Ole Bones' stall just like a house was kept. He would come in with his white gloves on and rub his hands across Exterminator's back. If there was any dirt on his gloves, I'd have to clean him all over again." [4]

Kilmer proudly gave Finney a tour of the house, which Finney described as a "comfortable, rambling, wooden structure with a delightful outlook over the water..." On its walls hung Kilmer's collection of antiques and rare equine paintings, particularly one of Sun Briar by Konrad. Less than six weeks later, it was all gone.

Kilmer had installed an elaborate fire-fighting system, possibly during the mansion's renovation. As described by historian Floyd West: "There were three large water towers. One provided water and fire protection for the mansion, one at the farm and one near the boarding house. The main tank had 4" water lines going to all the stables where fire stations with hoses and nozzles were strategically located."

For some reason, perhaps for maintenance or repair, the water was turned off on the night of February 5, 1938 when fire broke out. The Kilmers were alerted in time to escape with a few things they could grab, but the wooden house went quickly and Willis Kilmer stood in the damp cold night watching it go. He never really recovered.

Sun Briar had done quite well since his days on the racetrack, having sired the winners of more than two million dollars, and ranked among the top twenty sires eight times. Sun Briar's best get, and the best horse Kilmer ever bred, was Sun Beau. The 1925 foal retired in 1931 as the world's leading money winner with $376,744 and thirty-three victories in seventy-four starts. Another member of that crop was Reigh Count, a son of Sun Briar's brother, Sunreigh, and the cause of Henry McDaniel's third trip through Kilmer's revolving door in 1927.

J.K.L. Ross' retirement from racing the year before left McDaniel temporarily available. When Kilmer dangled a record salary of $20,000 plus bonuses in front of him, McDaniel accepted, but not without some doubts. It's possible the man has mellowed, he thought. Their differences erupted almost immediately. McDaniel was impressed with Reigh Count, but Kilmer wanted to sell him. McDaniel argued; Kilmer dug in his heels and sold him anyway to Mrs. John Hertz for a "modest" price. McDaniel quit. A trainer had to have some input.

Reigh Count went on to be ranked atop the juvenile division, and in 1928, won the Kentucky Derby and the Saratoga and Jockey Club Gold cups, among others, and went on to sire the immortal Count Fleet, the 1943 Triple Crown winner.

Kilmer never got over the need to compete with his trainers. Sun Beau went through eleven changes during his seventy-four race career. Sometimes the trainers quit under the strain. Too often their dismissal came out of the blue. Like the day in July 1931, when

Andy Schuttinger learned he'd been fired.

"Last week Jack Whyte, trainer of the Canadian division of the horses of Willis Sharpe Kilmer, went to Arlington Park, Chicago, and presented to Andrew Schuttinger, trainer of Sun Beau and others of the Kilmer first string, a letter from Mr. Kilmer. The letter informed Mr. Schuttinger that Mr. Whyte was to replace him immediately as trainer of the main stable...Mr. Kilmer has changed trainers so often that sports writers have lost count." [5]

Kilmer was at his Sky Lake estate in the mountains near Binghamton when he "galloped off on a pale Horse" on July 12, 1940. "His passing," wrote Neil Newman in *The Thoroughbred Record*, "removes from the scene one of the pillars of racing and breeding." Newman, a longtime friend, admitted Kilmer often offended some by his brusque manner, "...but this was merely a shield and hid a heart of gold. His benefactions were numerous and carefully hidden from the public — I have personal knowledge of many of them which I do not feel at liberty to put down in black and white."

The dispersal of the Kilmer stable that October 30

was highly successful. The 101 head of breeding stock brought an average of $2,230 each. Sun Beau would later be leased to Virginia horseman Christopher Chenery; and according to Kilmer's instructions, twenty-five-year-old Sun Briar was pensioned, and the eleven-year-old broodmare Suntica was retained by Mrs. Kilmer and produced four more foals. Kilmer also stipulated that Exterminator, who had been moved to Court Manor after the fire, be well cared for the rest of his life. Altogether, among the three facilities, some four hundred horses were sold. Mrs. Kilmer kept a few to race under her own colors.

The two patriarchs returned to Sun Briar Court in mid-June of 1942, a move that was noticed by the *Daily Mirror*'s Bob Considine.

"The swaybacked principals in one of the great and engaging stories of the turf, Exterminator and Sun Briar, came home to Binghamton, N.Y. the other day to live out the rest of their days and years in a kind of horse heaven on earth. Each is 27...

"...there was only one Exterminator. He'll be boss at the Binghamton 'old man's home,' and his faithful old playmate, Peanuts, a Shetland pony almost as old as he is, will carry out his orders..."

Sun Briar died on Monday, October 18, 1943. Because of a Binghamton ordinance prohibiting burying animals within city limits, he was interred in a pet cemetery south of town, leaving space for his companions.

Sixteen days before, Exterminator had made the second of two trips back to a racetrack. In 1941, he was vanned from Court Manor to Baltimore to commemorate the two mile and seventy yard Exterminator Handicap. Pimlico's young president and champion of distance racing, Alfred Gwynne Vanderbilt, had established the race the year before, but the Kilmer dispersal had prevented getting Exterminator there.

"You should have seen the old boy at the race," Mike Terry later recalled. "There must have been 38,000 people in the stands, and when Exterminator came out, they started to clap and yell. My horse sort of bowed to them and nodded his head.

"While we were walking along, a woman came dashing out and threw her arms around Slim's neck...she kept saying, 'I'm gonna follow him today.

He won me my home in Maryland once.' " And she was still hanging on to him when Terry led Exterminator into the paddock.

"We thought sure 'Old Bones' would get all heated up watching those other horses race," said Terry, "but he just put his ears back and turned around in that [in]field so he could see the leaders race by. He watched that whole race, two miles it was, too, as calmly as can be." [6]

The race was a good one, captured in world-record time by a seven-year-old Argentinian named Filisteo. But Exterminator stole the show. *Philadelphia Inquirer* correspondent Cy Peterman wrote that there wasn't a racer that day "who could have carried Old Bones' blanket." But the strain was getting to him. "...he looked rather like an old man, tired at last from his outing. He'd been to the big city, however, and had his final fling — and for a horse, of 26 summers, that's quite a journey's end."

The old man had one more fling in him — to Belmont Park on October 2, 1943. Normally it would have been Futurity Day, enough to bring in a crowd itself. But it was not quite two years since the attack on Pearl Harbor, which the American fleets were still trying to overcome, so this was "Back the Attack Day" and admission was by the purchase of War Bonds only. It was a huge success, the gate totaling ten million dollars. Likely a groom handled Peanuts at Pimlico, but Belmont decided to draw the name of some lucky youngster to lead the pony during the parade. Fourteen-year-old Bill Cherry won the draw and discovered to his surprise that forty inches packaged in a Shetland pony is more than a handful.

"I envied the man handling Exterminator," Cherry told this writer in a telephone interview. "I'm sure it was Milford Bray. I had a lot of trouble with Peanuts. I had such a hard time holding him, I asked Bray if we could change places and he just laughed. I really earned that forty, fifty dollars, whatever it was that day.

"Exterminator was grand looking," he continued, "...and the groom could do anything with him. But Exterminator did have a few little quirks. He wouldn't go in the stall without that pony. And his groom warned me, 'Don't walk into the stall until I go first.'"

As long as Exterminator had the pony with him, he

was gentle as a lamb, especially around children. Youngsters stopped by Sun Briar Court every day after school with such regularity the gelding knew what time they should be there. "He moped until the children came," said Mrs. Kilmer. Perhaps it was their bringing him "presents" of his favorite treats that she decided to give him a birthday party. Man o' War had a party back in '38, when he turned twenty-one. Announcer Clem McCarthy broadcast Man o' War's party coast-to-coast, and distinguished guests, including Kentucky governor Happy Chandler, sipped champagne.

No broadcast for Exterminator's party. No governor. Children and adults sipped punch and enjoyed cake and ice cream while Old Bones and Peanuts gobbled up creations made from a mash of oats and greens with large carrots for candles. It was downright difficult to tell who had the better time, Exterminator or the kids. So Mrs. Kilmer decided to hold one every year on the Sunday nearest his May 30 birthday.

By the time Exterminator celebrated his thirtieth in late May, 1945, the war in Europe had been over some three weeks, and four months later, on September 2,

Japan formally surrendered. For the second time in his life, Exterminator lived in a world recovering from global conflict.

EXTERMINATOR

EPILOGUE

"a very great story for a little town"

One day in mid-August of 1945, after having his customary roll in the paddock, Exterminator was unable to get to his feet without help. For the first time, Mike Terry was struck with Exterminator's imminent mortality.

The end came six weeks later.

Shortly after two in the morning of September 26, the barn's night-watchman awakened Terry. "Old Slim can't get up." As Terry hurried to the stable, a tightness gripped his chest.

Exterminator was conscious, but all efforts to get him up were futile. He was shutting down. "Get Peanuts out of here," Terry ordered. The pony was frantic, squealing and running around the stall, now and then stopping to nudge the big horse. It took several men to finally neutralize the kicking hind end long enough to get the pony into another stall.

Around 3:30 a.m., with his head in Terry's lap, Exterminator breathed his last. Word spread so quickly on this Wednesday that by the time the casket, which Mrs. Kilmer had ordered a few months earlier from a Virginia firm, was loaded onto a flatbed truck and Exterminator prepared for removal, a crowd was already gathered at Sun Briar Court, including teary-eyed children, who just four months earlier had helped Old Bones celebrate his birthday, and friends of the Kilmers, some of whom were taking care of preparing the gravesite.

Mike Terry did what he could. But when the time came to remove the body, he said his goodbyes and retreated to his cottage to take a nap. He was forty-six, and most of those years had been spent around Thoroughbreds, most of which as Kilmer's head groom. He had a tough leathery exterior defending him from the inevitable heartaches. Sun Briar's death had breached those defenses. And now Exterminator's.

Old Bones was wrapped in a blanket and lowered by a mechanical lift into the casket. Then the truck and several cars pulled out of Sun Briar Court and turned right onto Riverside Drive. Shortly afterwards, Terry agreed to talk with *Binghamton Press* reporter Louise Priore. He fingered the noseband on Exterminator's halter. "It was on him when he died, and I cleaned it just before you came." It was his now. "I couldn't bear to see him taken away from the stable," the Charlottesville, Virginia, native drawled softly.

"What am I going to do now? Well, I'll miss Slim, all right, but there's things for me to do around here. That's Peanuts' stall now." Then he excused himself and began clearing out the stall.

After crossing the Susquehanna River, the route to the pet cemetery follows Morgan Road, winds past Ross Park, ascends a hill, and turns onto Gardner Road. The nine acres had been purchased several years earlier by two local veterinarian brothers, John and Bill LaFrance, so residents would have an alternative to the city dump for their pets. What markers existed were flat, save one: a four-foot high granite slab standing on the highest ground, etched with the left profile of a horse head, below which was Sun Briar's name and the date, 1915-1943.

Following a brief, solemn ceremony, the greatest cup horse that ever ran, a claim backed up by the

1936 *American Racing Manual*, was laid to his well-deserved rest.

The tributes came quickly. Exterminator's death put a "footnote to the career of a horse that stirred more genuine affection in the hearts of men than any other thoroughbred the American turf has ever known," said his obituary in *The Thoroughbred Record* three days later.

"...he won every kind of race the track secretaries could think up...They piled weight on him that would have made a mule driver apologize to a mountain burro, and sent him out to take on the best at their favorite distances...

"...the American turf is a far greater, richer institution for his having passed by." The horse is buried, Jack Shay wrote in the *Binghamton Press*, "but what he did will never be entombed. It will run freely, as easily as the horse himself once ran, alive, in the memories of years past, through all the time yet to come." Both Matt Winn and the great sports writer Grantland Rice said Exterminator was the greatest all-around horse they ever saw.

"He was good because he was true," said Mrs. Kilmer years later. "Of course, I'm a sentimentalist, but

I saw what he did. It's a rare thing having a horse like that. His was a very great story for a little town."

All of the names are on that monument in the old LaFrance cemetery: Sun Briar, 1915-1943; Exterminator, 1915-1945; and Suntica, 1929-1947. And one by one, the roster of those in Exterminator's life shortened.

Henry McDaniel died on January 24, 1948, in a Florida hospital after a short illness and more than sixty active years in the business. On November 1, 1947, he sent his last horse, Nassau, to the post and won. "Uncle" Henry was inducted into the Racing Hall of Fame in 1956.

Mrs. Kilmer sold Sun Briar Court to a developer in 1948, and immediately its death throes could be heard. Tile by tile, rock by rock, the stable where Exterminator and Sun Briar lived came down. By 1965 Sun Briar Court was but a memory and a line of expensive homes. Only two structures remain: the clubhouse, where once the artifacts from Sun Briar's juvenile championship were displayed, now part of the Lourdes Hospital; and Kilmer's magnificent castle-like stone residence at 9 Riverside Drive, today a Jewish synagogue.

On February 11, 1949, J. Cal Milam passed at age seventy-six. He had been in ill health for some time and had to retire from training in 1939. Then it was a gap to October 25, 1972, when William "Big Bill" Knapp was struck by a car while walking near his home in Queens, Long Island. He died the next day at eighty-four. He had been inducted into the Hall of Fame in 1969.

Mrs. Kilmer had remarried in 1949, becoming Mrs. Eben Howes Ellison Jr. Widowed a second time in 1964, she spent most of her life as one of Binghamton's best-loved philanthropists. When she died on October 2, 1982, she was living in a multi-story luxury apartment building at 5 Riverside Drive, overlooking the home she had shared with Willis.

Exterminator was inducted into the Hall of Fame in 1957. Jeanne Williams, a Binghamton native of Ukrainian heritage who grew up with the lore of Exterminator, passed along an old Russian saying: "As long as you are remembered, you live."

Exterminator lives.

EXTERMINATOR

POSTSCRIPT

One of the best-known racing records is that of Exterminator. A hundred starts, half of them wins, has a nice, rounded-off ring to it. "There is a kind of mythology surrounding Exterminator's racing record, like there's something special about a hundred starts and fifty wins..." said Paula Welch, who was special projects editor at *Daily Racing Form* and instrumental in compiling their glorious volume, *Champions*. But should Exterminator's record be based on myth or fact? Should his record show sixteen unplaced finishes instead of fifteen?

It has to do with the "race" against the clock at Hawthorne in 1922, which *The Thoroughbred Record* described as an exhibition. According to John Hervey, who saw the event and was adamant about the race not counting, the owners of Hawthorne were in need of "something special in the way of an attraction…" and invited Exterminator "for an exhibition gallop. Ordinarily, such an affair would receive no official record. But under the circumstances, to 'boost' the meeting as much as possible, it was dignified with a chart and went onto 'the books.' As a matter of strict fact, therefore," Hervey concluded, "Exterminator ran 99 races — actual contests."

Back in the 1960s, when I first became really fascinated by Exterminator, I puzzled over this "race." How could he — being the only runner — be charged with finishing worse than third? And should such an event as this even be counted as a start? In e-mail correspondence of February 2, 2002, Paula Welch wrote, "It's my opinion that this time trial should not have been counted as an official start."

You may ask what difference one race makes. Who wouldn't, given the opportunity, delete the Sanford Memorial from Man o' War's record, or the Kentucky Derby from Native Dancer's? What Secretariat devotee wouldn't love to throw out his first race, the only unplaced finish in his career?

But could Exterminator's record even be changed

after all this time? The fact is, somewhere down the line his record was changed to show the error! Many early sources indicate his actually winning fifty of ninety-nine starts and with fifteen unplaced efforts.

His obituary in the *Binghamton Press* of August 26, 1945, recounted the gelding's race record as fifty wins in ninety-nine starts. Early editions of the *American Racing Manual* show four unplaced finishes in 1922. John McEvoy, who for fifteen years was Midwest editor for *Daily Racing Form*, told this writer: "I have no idea why a race against time would appear in Exterminator's career record as a unplaced finish. This should not be."

Paula Welch wrote on February 1, 2002: "I think it's very valid to call the statistic into question; but who is the final judge?" Perhaps the readers and historians. At any rate I tender Exterminator's corrected race record here.

Has a nice ring to it, I think.

Year	Age	Starts	Won	2nd	3rd	Unplaced
1917	2	4	2	0	0	2
1918	3	15	7	4	3	1
1919	4	21	9	6	3	3
1920	5	17	10	3	2	2
1921	6	16	8	2	5	1
1922	7	16	10	1	1	4
1923	8	3	1	1	1	0
1924	9	7	3	0	2	2
Total		**99**	**50**	**17**	**17**	**15**

EXTERMINATOR's
PEDIGREE

		Wisdom
	Sir Hugo, 1889	Manoeuvre
White Knight, 1895		
	Whitelock, 1881	Wenlock
		White Heather
McGEE (GB), b, 1900		
		Newminster
	Hermit, 1864	Seclusion
Remorse, 1876		
	Vex, 1865	Vedette
EXTERMINATOR, chestnut gelding, 1915		Flying Duchess
		Virgil
	Hindoo, 1878	Florence
Jim Gore, 1884		
	Katie, 1872	Phaeton
FAIR EMPRESS, blk, 1899		Mare by War Dance
	Pirate of Penzance, 1882	Prince Charlie
		Plunder
Merrythought, 1893		
	Raybelle, 1889	Rayon d'Or
		Blue Grass Belle

EXTERMINATOR's RACE RECORD

Exterminator — ch. g. 1915, by McGee (White Knight)–Fair Empress, by Jim Gore — **Lifetime record: 100 50 17 17 $252,996**

Own.– W.S. Kilmer
Br.– F.D. Knight (Ky)
Tr.– H. McDaniel

21Jun24-5Dor	gd	1$\frac{1}{16}$	:23^{2} :47^{4} 1:13^{2} 1:47	3↑ Queen's Hotel H 3k	4	3	$3^{1\frac{1}{4}}$	$3^{\frac{3}{4}}$	$4^{2\frac{1}{2}}$	$3^{5\frac{1}{2}}$	Wallace J	113	w	*1.30	84-13	SpotCash128$^{2\frac{1}{2}}$ForestLor103^{3}Extrmntor113^{nk}	Pulled up lame	5
7Jun24-6BB	gd	1	:23^{2} :47^{3} 1:13^{2} 1:39^{4}	3↑ Alw 1000	1	4	$2^{1\frac{1}{2}}$	2^{1}	2^{2}	1^{1}	Wallace J	111	w	1.85	90-14	Exterminator111^{1}Golden Rule113^{4}Opperman111^{6}	Handily	5
1May24-6Pim	fst	1	:24^{2} :48^{3} 1:13 1:38^{3}	3↑ Handicap 2000	4	5	$4^{2\frac{1}{2}}$	$5^{5\frac{1}{4}}$	$4^{6\frac{1}{4}}$	$3^{10\frac{1}{2}}$	Johnson A	126	w	4.80	84-11	Martingale120$^{\frac{1}{2}}$SpicndSpn106^{10}Extrmntor126^{1}	Always outrun	6
19Apr24-5HdG	hy	1$\frac{1}{16}$	:23^{2} :48^{2} 1:15^{3} 1:49^{2}	3↑ Philadelphia H 5.1k	6	5	$6^{5\frac{1}{2}}$	6^{3}	$5^{6\frac{3}{4}}$	$5^{8\frac{1}{4}}$	Johnson A	125	w	*1.20e	69-25	SpotCash111^{hd}FlintStone118^{nk}NewHampshire112^{4}	No mishap	6
17Apr24-5HdG	fst	1 70	:24^{4} :49 1:14 1:44	3↑ Alw 2000	2	2	$2^{1\frac{1}{2}}$	1^{hd}	1^{hd}	$1^{\frac{1}{2}}$	Walls P	107	w	*.50	92-11	Exterminator107$^{\frac{1}{2}}$GoldenSpher103$^{\frac{1}{2}}$SttngSun106^{15}	Ridden out	5
30Mar24-6Tij	fst	1$\frac{1}{4}$	:47^{4} 1:12^{4} 1:39 2:05^{2}	3↑ Coffroth H 51k	11	7	$6^{5\frac{3}{4}}$	$5^{4\frac{1}{4}}$	5^{3}	$4^{1\frac{1}{2}}$	Johnson A	130	w	*1.60e	97-14	Runstar123^{no}Osprey123^{no}CherryTree117$^{1\frac{1}{2}}$	Challenged,tired	18
17Feb24-4Tij	fst	1 70	:24^{1} :48^{3} 1:13^{3} 1:44^{3}	4↑ Alw 700	4	2	$2^{\frac{3}{4}}$	2^{1}	1^{1}	1^{1}	Johnson A	113	w	*.30	89-12	Extermintor113^{1}Suprcrgo116^{1}VnPtrck101^{1}	Gentle hand ride	5
	Previously trained by W. Shields																	
28Apr23-5HdG	my	1 70	:24^{2} :49^{3} 1:14^{3} 1:45^{2}	3↑ Handicap 2500	3	4	$3^{1\frac{1}{2}}$	2^{1}	$2^{\frac{1}{2}}$	2no	Johnson A	132	w	*1.10	85-21	Chickvl101^{no}Extrmntor132^{1}PulJons108^{10}	Getting to winner	5
21Apr23-5HdG	fst	1$\frac{1}{16}$	:24 :48 1:12^{3} 1:45^{4}	3↑ Philadelphia H 5.1k	2	4	$5^{3\frac{1}{2}}$	$4^{2\frac{1}{4}}$	$2^{\frac{3}{4}}$	1^{nk}	McAtee L	129	w	*.80	95-10	Exterminator129^{nk}Paul Jones109^{2}Fair Phantom107^{nk}	Gamely	6
16Apr23-4HdG	my	6f	:24 :49 1:15	3↑ Harford H 5.1k	4	5	6^{4}	$6^{2\frac{3}{4}}$	$4^{2\frac{1}{2}}$	$3^{1\frac{1}{4}}$	Sande E	132	w	3.70	80-32	Blazes106^{nk}Careful116$^{\frac{1}{2}}$Exterminator132^{6}	Finished fast	8
	Previously trained by E. Wayland																	
11Nov22-4Pim	fst	2$\frac{1}{4}$	:50 2:34 3:04 3:53^{2}	3↑ Pim Cup H 10k	5	2	2^{hd}	4^{6}	4^{18}	$3^{31\frac{1}{2}}$	Marineli B	126	w	*.65	66-13	CaptanAlcock106$^{1\frac{1}{2}}$PulJons99^{30}Extrmntor126^{100}	Forced pace	5
28Oct22-5Lrl	fst	1$\frac{1}{4}$	:47 1:12^{2} 1:38^{2} 2:04^{4}	3↑ Washington H 28k	8	5	5^{4}	$4^{4\frac{1}{2}}$	4^{5}	$4^{3\frac{1}{2}}$	Johnson A	132	w	*.90	82-17	Oceanic104$^{\frac{1}{2}}$Lucky Hour120^{2}Paragon II121^{1}	Finished fast	8
21Oct22-5Lrl	fst	1	:24^{4} :49 1:14 1:40	2↑ Laurel 13k	1	5	5^{3}	4^{2}	$3^{1\frac{1}{2}}$	$1^{2\frac{1}{2}}$	Johnson A	132	w	2.25	88-15	Extermintor132$^{2\frac{1}{2}}$[D]PrgonII125$^{1\frac{1}{2}}$Trystr123^{hd}	Won easing up	8
14Oct22-4Lrl	fst	6f	:23 :47 1:12^{4}	3↑ Handicap 2000	8	2	$8^{6\frac{3}{4}}$	$6^{4\frac{1}{2}}$	6^{5}	$4^{1\frac{1}{2}}$	Johnson A	133	w	*2.25	92-16	CalamityJane113^{hd}OnWatch124^{1}TipptyWtcht112$^{\frac{1}{2}}$	Steady gain	8
30Sep22-5Haw	fst	1$\frac{1}{4}$	:51^{4} 1:18^{3} 1:45^{1} 2:10	Special	-	1	1	1	1	1	Johnson A	126	w	-	73-19	Exterminator126	Good run	1
	Race against time																	
20Sep22-5OW	fst	1$\frac{1}{4}$	:46^{3} 1:11^{3} 1:38^{2} 2:05^{1}	3↑ Toronto Aut Cup H 16k	5	5	$5^{3\frac{3}{4}}$	$4^{2\frac{1}{2}}$	$3^{\frac{1}{2}}$	$1^{1\frac{1}{2}}$	Johnson A	132	w	*.80	95-09	Exterminator132$^{1\frac{1}{2}}$Guy102^{hd}BitofWhit100^{1}	Rated,going away	8
31Aug22-4Sar	gd	1$\frac{3}{4}$	:50 2:10 2:35 3:00^{2}	3↑ Sar Cup 8.3k	1	1	1^{1}	1^{1}	1^{1}	1^{nk}	Johnson A	126	w	1.40	80-18	Exterminatr126^{nk}MdHttr126^{12}BonHomm126	Outstayed rivals	3
1Aug22-4Sar	fst	1$\frac{1}{4}$	:48^{1} 1:12^{3} 1:38 2:03^{1}	3↑ Saratoga H 9.2k	1	4	5^{2}	$5^{3\frac{1}{2}}$	5^{7}	$5^{10\frac{1}{4}}$	Johnson A	137	w	5.00	83-09	Grey Lag130$^{\frac{1}{2}}$Bon Homme109$^{1\frac{1}{4}}$Prudery114^{6}	Hard ridden	5
4Jly22-5Lat	gd	1$\frac{1}{2}$	:48^{2} 1:12^{2} 2:04^{1} 2:30^{2}	3↑ Independence H 18k	2	4	$4^{4\frac{1}{2}}$	$5^{9\frac{1}{2}}$	6^{8}	6^{12}	Johnson A	140	w	*.90	84-14	Firebrand116^{3}Devastation102^{6}Minto II116^{1}		8
	Appeared in distress after mile																	
16Jun22-4Aqu	fst	1$\frac{1}{8}$	:47^{3} 1:12^{3} 1:37 1:50	3↑ Brooklyn H 9.8k	2	3	3^{2}	$2^{\frac{1}{2}}$	2^{hd}	1^{hd}	Johnson A	135	w	1.50	95-10	Exterminator135^{hd}GreyLag126^{4}PollyAnn103^{hd}	Strong finish	5
13Jun22-4Bel	fst	1$\frac{1}{16}$	:23^{4} :48 1:13^{1} 1:44	3↑ Handicap 1635	5	4	$2^{1\frac{1}{2}}$	2^{2}	1^{1}	$1^{1\frac{1}{2}}$	Johnson A	135	w	1.40	96-12	Exterminator135$^{1\frac{1}{2}}$Mad Hatter128^{6}Devastation102^{nk}	Rated	6
5Jun22-4Bel	gd	1$\frac{1}{8}$	:47 1:12^{2} 1:38^{2} 1:52^{2}	3↑ Handicap 1470	2	1	1no	$1^{\frac{1}{2}}$	$1^{\frac{1}{2}}$	$1^{\frac{1}{2}}$	Johnson A	133	w	*.07	83-11	Exterminator133$^{\frac{1}{2}}$Be Frank107	Won hard held	2
27May22-5CD	sl	1$\frac{1}{4}$	:48 1:12^{2} 1:38^{2} 2:04^{2}	3↑ Kentucky H 12k	1	2	2^{hd}	1^{1}	$1^{1\frac{1}{2}}$	$1^{1\frac{1}{2}}$	Johnson A	138	w	*.45	94-15	Exterminator138$^{1\frac{1}{2}}$Firebrand119^{5}Blarney Stone95^{8}	Easily	4
20May22-5CD	fst	1$\frac{1}{8}$	:47^{1} 1:12 1:37 1:50	3↑ Clark H 13k	5	4	$5^{1\frac{1}{2}}$	2^{nk}	$1^{\frac{1}{2}}$	$1^{1\frac{1}{2}}$	Johnson A	133	w	*.60	99-10	Exterminator133$^{1\frac{1}{2}}$Lady Madcap111^{1}Rouleau107^{4}	Drew away	9
6May22-6Pim	sl	1$\frac{1}{16}$	:24^{3} :49^{3} 1:14 1:45^{4}	3↑ Pim Spring H 5.6k	3	2	2^{1}	1^{nk}	1^{hd}	1^{hd}	Johnson A	133	w	*.75	97-18	Exterminator133^{hd}Boniface125^{10}Registrar102^{2}	Hard drive	7
22Apr22-5HdG	fst	1$\frac{1}{16}$	:24^{4} :48^{3} 1:14^{1} 1:45	3↑ Philadelphia H 5.5k	2	2	$3^{1\frac{1}{4}}$	$3^{1\frac{1}{2}}$	2^{hd}	2no	Johnson A	133	w	*.65	99-09	Boniface122^{no}Exterminator133^{6}BungaBuck110^{nk}	Cut off $\frac{3}{8}$	6
15Apr22-4HdG	hy	6f	:23^{4} :48^{1} 1:14^{1}	3↑ Harford H 5.2k	7	4	$6^{4\frac{1}{2}}$	4^{3}	4^{2}	1^{1}	Johnson A	132	wb	4.95	85-24	Exterminator132^{1}Billy Kelly132^{1}Dexterous102^{1}	Going away	12
	Previously trained by W. Knapp																	
12Nov21-5Pim	hy	2$\frac{1}{4}$	:55 2:46^{2} 3:12 4:08^{1}	3↑ Pim Cup H 9.8k	1	1	$1^{\frac{1}{2}}$	$1^{\frac{1}{2}}$	1^{hd}	1^{hd}	Johnson A	126	w	*.70	--	Exterminator126^{hd}Boniface121^{20}Lady Emmeline96	Held on	3
29Oct21-5Lxt	fst	1$\frac{1}{2}$	:50^{2} 1:16^{1} 2:07 2:31^{3}	3↑ Lex Cup H 6.2k	5	3	3^{3}	2^{3}	$3^{2\frac{1}{2}}$	$3^{6\frac{1}{2}}$	Johnson A	135	w	*.80	84-10	Firbrnd118$^{1\frac{1}{2}}$UntdVrd105^{5}Extrmntor135^{2}	Tired under impost	5
22Oct21-4Lrl	fst	1$\frac{1}{4}$	:47^{1} 1:12 1:38^{2} 2:04^{2}	3↑ Handicap 2038	6	3	3^{7}	3^{4}	2^{nk}	1^{1}	Johnson A	132	w	*1.65	88-14	Exterminator132^{1}My Dear115$^{1\frac{1}{2}}$Bygone Days96$^{1\frac{1}{2}}$	Driving	6

EXTERMINATOR's RACE RECORD CONTINUED

8Oct21-4Lrl	sly 1½	:483 1:141 2:06 2:35	3↑ Annapolis H 12k	6	4	1hd	21	33	38½	Kelsay W	135	w	*2.15	64-23	ThePorter1202½MyDer1146Extrmntr1351½	Eased when beaten	8
24Sep21-5OW	fst 1¼	:48 1:132 1:383 2:051	3↑ Toronto Aut Cup H 7.9k	6	4	43½	2½	1½	1nk	Kelsay W	137	w	*1.40	95-12	Exterminator137nkMy Dear1172Golden Sphere1061	Gamely	9
16Sep21-4Bel	fst 2	:493 2:352 3:02 3:291	3↑ Autumn Gold Cup H 5.7k	2	2	1hd	11	13	16	Kelsay W	130	w	*.33	63-19	Exterminator1306Bellsolar104	In a canter	2
31Aug21-4Sar	sl 1¾	:554 2:132 2:393 3:043	3↑ Sar Cup 4.5k	-	1	1	1	1	1	Kelsay W	126	w	-	59-22	Exterminator126	Galloped	1
	Walkover																
27Aug21-4Sar	fst 1 3/16	:472 1:114 1:373 1:572	3↑ Merchants & Cits H 8.7k	6	5	51¾	21	1½	11	Kelsay W	130	w	6.00	91-10	Exterminator1301MadHattr132¾Bllsolr104hd	Outside,gamely	7
	Previously trained by F. Curtis																
12Jly21-4Wnr	fst 1⅛	:471 1:12 1:382 1:512	3↑ Frontier H 12k	7	4	51¾	32½	31½	32	Simpson R	132	w	4.20	97-07	BestPal1191½IrishKiss108½Extrmntor1328	Closed with rush	8
9Jly21-5Lat	fst 1 3/16	:473 1:122 1:373 1:561	3↑ Daniel Boone H 14k	7	4	21	1½	21½	32	Haynes E	135	w	2.20	100-08	Best Pal1191La Rablee1061Exterminator1356		8
	Cut off by winner final ⅛																
4Jly21-5Lat	fst 1½	:493 1:141 2:052 2:301	3↑ Independence H 19k	5	3	32	21	1½	11	Haynes E	130	w	*.55	97-07	Exterminator1301Woodtrap1111½La Rablee1086	Handily	7
	Previously trained by W. McDaniel																
17Jun21-4Aqu	gd 1⅛	:462 1:11 1:362 1:494	3↑ Brooklyn H 9.8k	10	7	74	42½	42½	33	Ensor L	129	w	4.00	94-08	GreyLag1121½JohnP.Grier1241½Extrmntor1291	Inside,gamely	11
4Jun21-4Bel	fst 1¼	:473 1:12 1:361 2:021	3↑ Suburban H 11k	8	5	58½	59½	59½	58¾	Johnson A	133	w	*1.20	80-09	Audacious120¾MadHattr1306SennngsPrk110no	Always outrun	8
21May21-4Jam	fst 1⅛	:48 1:123 1:372 1:50	3↑ Long Beach H 5.8k	3	2	21½	1hd	1½	1¾	Johnson A	130	w	*1.00	106-03	Exterminator130¾Mad Hatter1305Cirrus1287	Drew clear	4
14May21-4Jam	my 1 1/16	:233 :481 1:14 1:471	3↑ Excelsior H 10k	1	5	53	42½	31½	21	Johnson A	129	w	3.60	89-15	Blazes1181Exterminator1296Naturalist126¾	Slow late gain	7
7May21-4Jam	fst 1 1/16	:233 :472 1:12 1:45	3↑ Kings County H 6.1k	3	3	44½	35	25	23	Haynes E	129	w	2.20	98-08	MadHatter1243Extrmintr1293YllowHnd1101½	Closed gamely	5
12Nov20-4Pim	fst 2¼	:472 2:321 2:583 3:53	3↑ Pim Cup H 10k	2	3	21	11	1½	1no	Ensor L	126	w	*.75	20- -	Exterminator126noBonifc11410PulJons110.56	Rated,all out	7
8Nov20-4Pim	fst 1½	:483 1:142 2:051 2:313	3↑ Bowie H 11k	3	7	73½	53½	63¾	53½	Fairbrother C	135	w	2.80	94-08	Mad Hatter120noBoniface1221½The Porter128no	In a pocket	9
20Oct20-5OW	hy 2¼	:513 2:393 3:094 4:044	3↑ Ont Jockey Club Cup 7.7k	1	1	22	22	1nk	11¼	Fairbrother C	134	w	*.15	49-26	Exterminator1341¼Bondage1106St. Germain901½	Easily	4
25Sep20-5OW	fst 1¼	:482 1:133 1:394 2:042	3↑ Toronto Aut Cup 7.8k	4	2	11	11	1½	1hd	Fairbrother C	132	w	*.25	99-10	Exterminator132hdMy Dear9212Bondage1081	Driving	5
	Previously trained by J.S. Healey																
15Sep20-4Bel	fst 2	:482 2:293 3:214	3↑ Autumn Gold Cup 6.3k	2	3	32½	32	2½	1hd	Fairbrother C	128	w	*.70	- -	Exterminator128hdDamask982½Cleopatra105	Rated,driving	3
31Aug20-4Sar	sl 1¾	:502 2:043 2:294 2:562	3↑ Sar Cup 5.6k	2	1	11	11½	13	16	Fairbrother C	126	w	*.55	108-12	Exterminator1266Cleopatra111	Easily	2
28Aug20-4Wnr	fst 1 1/16	:23 :472 1:12 1:444	3↑ George Hendrie H 8.6k	4	3	31½	31¼	2½	11	Fairbrother C	131	w	*1.15	98-09	Exterminator1311Wildair1143My Dear95hd	Rated,going away	6
21Aug20-4Wnr	sl 1⅛	:48 1:132 1:384 1:511	3↑ Wnr Jockey Club H 11k	1	3	21½	21½	2nk	11¼	Fairbrother C	125	w	2.50	100-17	Exterminator1251¼Wildair11010Boniface130nk	Drew away	7
14Aug20-4Sar	gd 1⅛	:484 1:14 1:402 1:531	3↑ Champlain H 4.1k	1	4	21	31½	1½	21½	Schuttinger A	128	w	*2.20	82-19	Gnome1091½Extrminatr1281MadHatter1175	Inside,no match	7
2Aug20-4Sar	fst 1¼	:474 1:11 1:36 2:014	3↑ Saratoga H 6.7k	3	5	54½	21½	22½	22	Schuttinger A	126	w	7.00	100-06	SirBarton1292Exterminator1263Wildar1153	Gamely,no match	5
14Jly20-4Wnr	hy 1⅛	:492 1:182 1:47 2:011	3↑ Frontier H 12k	5	3	44	22	32½	32½	Davies T	127	w	*1.25	47-48	Slippery Elm109½The Porter1292Exterminator1275	Tired	8
3Jly20-4Aqu	my 1⅛	:481 1:124 1:373 1:501	3↑ Brookdale H 4.2k	2	3	3½	21	2½	11½	Schuttinger A	129	w	2.00	96-11	Exterminator1291½Cirrus1234Gladiator1126	Hard ridden	4
29Jun20-4Aqu	fst 1 1/16	:233 :462 1:11 1:44	3↑ Handicap 1290	3	3	34	33	31	1¾	Schuttinger A	126	w	3.00	101-18	Exterminator126¾Naturalist120½Wildair11412	Drew away	5
24Jun20-4Aqu	fst 1⅛	:47 1:11 1:363 1:50	3↑ Brooklyn H 7.3k	7	7	75	76	46	48¼	Schuttinger A	124	w	6.00	89-09	Cirrus108hdBoniface1228Mad Hatter115hd	Steadily	7
19Jun20-4Jam	gd 1⅛	:474 1:13 1:382 1:511	3↑ Long Beach H 4k	2	3	1½	11	11	11	Schuttinger A	119	w	2.20	102-06	Exterminator1191Cirrus1098Naturalist1203	Handily	5
5Jun20-4Bel	my 1¼	:52 1:163 1:432 2:093	3↑ Suburban H 7.8k	5	5	58½	46½	47	36	Rice T	123	w	*2.20	46-30	Paul Jones106hdBoniface1156Exterminator123½	Game try	5
29May20-5Bel	fst 1 1/16	:242 :48 1:13 1:443	3↑ Handicap 1605	4	3	21½	31	1½	2nk	Davies T	128	w	*2.00	97-10	Alibi107nkExterminator1282Sea Mint98no	Led,tired	5
	Previously trained by H. McDaniel																
13Nov19-4Pim	hy 2¼	:523 2:50 3:182 4:13	3↑ Pim Cup H 4.9k	1	1	22	14	12	14	Kummer C	121	w	*1.00	- -	Extrminatr1214RoycRools1058½Woodtrp1023	Won easing up	3
8Nov19-4Pim	fst 1½	:493 1:15 2:072 2:334	3↑ Bowie H 10k	5	3	52¾	55½	511	513½	Kummer C	128	w	2.90	73-11	Royce Rools1071½Cudgel1314Mad Hatter1132	Quit badly	5
18Oct19-5Lat	hy 2¼	:54 2:50 3:184 4:17	3↑ Lat Cup 8.7k	4	3	11	2hd	21½	22	Knapp W	134	w	*.45	- -	Be Frank1222Exterminator13420Legal10520	Tired	4

EXTERMINATOR's RACE RECORD CONTINUED

11Oct19-4Lrl	fst	1½	:473 1:13 2:033 2:293	3↑ Annapolis H 8.3k	3	3	34½	21	21½	2hd	Knapp W	128	w	2.05	107-06	Thunderclp108hdExtrmntor1283Cudgl1321	Getting to winner	5
3Oct19-3Lrl	fst	1 1/16	:242 :49 1:153 1:461	3↑ Alw 1200	2	1	11	1hd	1½	1nk	Knapp W	120	w	*.05	86-15	Exterminator120nkOrestes12010Douglass S.113	Hard ridden	3
27Sep19-5HdG	fst	1⅛	:471 1:122 1:373 1:50	3↑ Havre de Grace H 10k	5	6	64¾	4¾	41¾	2½	Knapp W	126	w	10.50	105-05	Cudgel129½Extrmntr126noSrBrton1242	Impeded,game finish	8
22Sep19-5HdG	fst	1 1/16	:24 :48 1:13 1:45	3↑ Purse 2527	1	2	22	21½	21	1¾	Schuttinger A	124	w	5.05	100-11	Exterminator124¾Cudgel1291Slippery Elm993	Gamely	5
11Sep19-4HdG	my	1 70	:25 :49 1:143 1:45	3↑ Harford County H 5.4k	4	2	3½	23	24	24	Schuttinger A	125	w	*.35	83-25	The Porter1214Exterminator1258Slippery Elm1033	No match	5
30Aug19-4Sar	sl	1¾	:48 2:07 2:32 2:58	3↑ Sar Cup 6.3k	3	1	11½	12	1½	11½	Schuttinger A	126	w	2.50	100-14	Extrmntr1261½Purchs11650ThTrump116	Challenged,drew away	3
23Aug19-4Sar	fst	1 3/16	:484 1:133 1:372 1:572	3↑ Merchants & Cits H 3.4k	1	1	11	2½	32½	33	Loftus J	126	w	*1.10e	90-08	Cudgel1321Star Master1222Exterminator1261½	No menace	5
9Aug19-4Sar	fst	1⅛	:48 1:123 1:371 1:50	3↑ Champlain H 3.4k	6	4	42¼	31	21	21	Loftus J	120	w	*.90e	106-09	SunBriar1281Extermintor120½Hollstr1151½	Not hard ridden	6
5Aug19-4Sar	fst	1	:232 :462 1:112 1:361	3↑ Delaware H 3.4k	6	5	44½	34	33½	31	Loftus J	121	w	*1.20e	99-08	FairyWand107hdSunBriar1281Exterminator121½	Fast finish	8
14Jun19-4Jam	fst	1 1/16	:244 :482 1:13 1:452	3↑ Excelsior H 4.8k	8	5	44½	45½	68	53¾	Loftus J	124	w	8.00	96-07	Naturalist1221Star Master1191Boniface108nk	No threat	8
7Jun19-4Bel	fst	1¼	:463 1:113 1:38 2:021	3↑ Suburban H 6.7k	1	4	57½	75¼	76¾	55¼	Rice T	128	w	5.00	84-16	Corn Tassel108nkSweep On1081½Boniface1073	Outrun	8
24May19-5CD	hy	1¼	:482 1:143 1:42 2:102	3↑ Kentucky H 14k	1	4	1½	1hd	1hd	31	Morys J	134	w	*2.15	64-31	Midway1221Beaverkill108noExterminator1342	Gamely	7
22May19-6CD	my	1	:25 :50 1:153 1:423	3↑ Handicap 1660	4	1	11½	12	11½	15	Morys J	134	w	*.60	74-39	Exterminator1345Flyaway97nkDrastic11210	Ridden out	4
15May19-4CD	fst	1	:25 :493 1:143 1:391	3↑ Alw 1800	4	1	1½	11	2hd	2no	Morys J	115	w	*.20	91-11	Under Fire103noExterminator1151½Bribed Voter1088		4
	Tight restraint,tired																	
8May19-4Lxt	my	1¼	:493 1:152 1:42 2:073	3↑ Camden H 2.5k	1	1	11	11	11	11	Morys J	132	w	*.35	81-28	Exterminator1321Midway118	Drawing away	2
1May19-4Lxt	hy	1 1/16	:243 :491 1:16 1:502	3↑ Ben Ali H 2.9k	4	3	21½	21½	11½	13	Morys J	124	w	*.60	70-33	Exterminator1243AmericanAc996Mdwy120hd	As rider pleased	5
31Mar19-4OP	fst	6f	:233 :48 1:124	3↑ Handicap 800	3	1	31½	32	1hd	11½	Haynes E	123	w	*1.00	96-09	Extrmntor1231½UltmThul1141½A.N.Akn1072	As rider pleased	6
22Mar19-4OP	fst	1 70	:242 :48 1:13 1:432	3↑ Handicap 800	2	2	2½	11½	11½	13	Schuttinger A	126	w	*.80	109-09	Exterminator1263Lucky B.1111½Drastic1113	Won eased up	4
28Nov18-5Lat	my	1 1/16	:243 :493 1:153 1:503	2↑ Handicap 2090	2	4	3½	12	14	12½	Loftus J	126	w	*.85	64-37	Exterminator1262½Drastic1046WrMchn1095	As rider pleased	8
23Nov18-5Lat	hy	2¼	:54 2:433 3:11 4:063	3↑ Lat Cup H 8.9k	6	6	11½	11	1hd	1no	Loftus J	121	w	*1.25	- -	Exterminator121noBeaverkill1105Moscowa1153	Gamely	6
12Nov18-4Pim	fst	1½	:49 1:142 2:043 2:311	3↑ Bowie H 12k	4	5	1½	24	22	31¼	Loftus J	120	w	6.85	102-06	GeorgeSmith130¾OmarKhayyam115½Extrmntr1206	Resolutely	15
6Nov18-4Pim	fst	1¼	:492 1:141 1:393 2:053	Pim Autumn H 5.4k	2	2	1hd	2hd	11	1½	Ensor L	118	w	3.20	99-09	Extrmntor118½Forground107nkThPortr1276	Outstayed rivals	5
31Oct18-4Lrl	hy	1⅛	:50 1:16 1:414 1:542	3↑ National H 3k	1	1	1nk	1nk	1nk	2hd	Knapp W	117	w	1.75	76-25	Midway117hdExterminator11720Tombolo98	Wide	3
26Oct18-6Lrl	fst	1⅛	:49 1:141 1:393 1:521	Ellicott City H 2.5k	5	1	1nk	13	11½	12½	Knapp W	113	w	*.30	87-08	Extermintor1132½Aurum104.51½RdSox105.5nk	Never extended	5
12Oct18-5Lrl	gd	1⅛	:49 1:143 1:402 1:512	3↑ Washington H 2.5k	3	1	1¾	22	32	33½	Knapp W	114	w	3.15	87-13	Midway111.52Cudgel1301½Exterminator113.51½	Tired badly	4
8Oct18-4Lrl	fst	1 1/16	:231 :464 1:124 1:441	Carrollton H 1.9k	4	1	1nk	1½	1½	1hd	Knapp W	118	w	12.70	96-11	Exterminator118hdThe Porter1265Sunny Slope1304	Gamely	4
4Oct18-4Lrl	fst	1 1/16	:24 :481 1:15 1:461	3↑ Alw 1408	4	1	12	11½	11	11	Kummer C	103	w	*.65	86-11	Exterminator1031Franklin1122John I. Day100no	Ridden out	4
30Aug18-4Sar	hy	1¼	:501 1:171 1:451 2:122	3↑ Handicap 1313	4	2	22	42½	47	39½	Knapp W	115	w	*2.20	48-34	Ticket1061½Bondage1068Extermntr1151½	Impeded by winner	5
17Aug18-4Sar	fst	1¼	:49 1:133 1:382 2:031	Travers 10k	2	2	44½	47	48	412	Schuttinger A	123	w	*1.10e	92-05	Sun Briar120hdJohren1266War Cloud1266	Outrun	4
3Aug18-4Sar	fst	1 3/16	:483 1:132 1:383 1:563	Kenner 4k	3	2	32½	33	31¾	22	Knapp W	129	w	5.00	105-02	Enfilade1142Exterminator129nkTippityWitcht1235	Game try	5
22Jun18-5Lat	fst	1½	:494 1:142 2:063 2:33	Lat Derby 12k	5	4	42½	35½	31½	22	Knapp W	124	w	8.75	85-11	Johren1272Exterminator124½Frecuttr1228	Hard ridden late	6
25May18-4BPT	fst	1		3↑ Turf and Field H .7k	-	-				21	Knapp W	122		*.45	- -	Kilts II1261Exterminator1221Square Dealer1262	Driving	6
	No time taken																	
11May18-5CD	my	1¼	:491 1:161 1:433 2:104	Ky Derby 18k	5	5	42½	1hd	2hd	11	Knapp W	114	w	29.60	63-25	Exterminator1141Escoba1178Viva America1134	Saved ground	8
	Previously owned and trained by J.C. Milam																	
26Jly17-2Knw	fst	5½f	:233 :473 1:004 1:071	Alw 800	3	7	64¾	45	66¾	4½	Morys J	112	w	*1.55	102-00	MissBryn112noOwnRoeO'Neil104½Salvstr112no	Finished fast	11
17Jly17-3Wnr	hy	5½f	:244 :51 1:052 1:13	Alw 800	2	6	43½	3nk	13	11	Kelsay W	105	w	7.85	63-41	Exterminator1051Fern Handley1031Lady Eileen1103	Handily	6
14Jly17-2Wnr	gd	5f	:23 :473 1:011	Alw 800	11	3	48	79¾	49	410	Morys J	105	w	14.35	84-18	Jack Hare Jr.1111High Cost1153Viva America1156	Bumped	11
30Jun17-1Lat	fst	6f	:233 :483 1:144	Md Sp Wt	2	2	12	12	11½	13	Morys J	109	w	5.20	81-12	Exterminator1093Mistress Polly1091Quito112½	Easily	12

References

Chapter 1

1. "Exterminator's Dam." *The Thoroughbred Record*. September 2, 1922. p.. 115.

2. West, Floyd R., Professor Emeritus of Biology, Broome Community College. "Willis Sharpe Kilmer and his Horses." Presented at the June 17, 1989, meeting of the Broome County Historical Society.

3. West. "Willis Sharpe Kilmer and Swamp Root Tonic. Opportunist or Benefactor?" Presented at the March 1999 meeting of the Broome County Historical Society. In 1892 Andral Kilmer sold his half to brother Jonas for $40,000 and for the remainder of his life devoted his energies to finding a cancer cure and running his three sanitariums.

4. West. Ibid.

5. Hollingsworth, Kent. *The Great Ones*. Lexington, Ky: The Blood-Horse (1970), p. 105.

Chapter 2

1. Jordan, Joe. *The Bluegrass Horse Country*. Lexington, Ky: Transylvania Press (1940), p. 98; and "J. Cal Milam, 76, Dies at Lexington." *The Blood-Horse*. February 19, 1949. p. 491.

2. Jordan. pp. 97-102. Merrick eventually lost his place in the Guinness book. The 1998 edition of the *Guinness Book of World Records* shows a gelding named Tango Duke (Australia) was foaled in 1935 and died in January of 1978 at the age of 43. p. 571.

3. 'Salvator.' "Exterminator and the Figure System." *The Thoroughbred Record*. September 23, 1922. p. 155.

4. Ibid.

5. "Kilmer to Import Racers." *The New York Times*. November 30, 1916.

6. Herring, Charles Griffin. *The Thoroughbred Record*. September 22, 1922. p. 151.

7. *Binghamton Press*. January 2, 1918. In *Hoofprints of the Century.*. Lexington, Ky: Record Publishing Co. (1975), pp. 198-199.

Chapter 3

1. Winn, Matt. *Down the Stretch*. New York: Smith & Durrell (1945), pp. 20-21.

2. Bergin, Charles A. *Lexington Leader*. April 7, 1918. p. 2.

3. Harrell, John. *Thoroughbred Times*. April 24, 1999, p. 29; Adams, Dr. O.R. *Lameness in Horses*. Philadelphia: Lea & Febiger (2001), pp. 233-240; and Thomas, Heather Smith. "Ringbone." *The Backstretch*. March/April 2001, pp. 24, 26-27. Thomas suggests that of the 'low' and 'high' ringbones, the former are the most debilitating.

4. Underwood, Thomas Rust. "Sun Briar to Make Debut." *Lexington Herald*. April 25, 1918.

5. Sources include: Moore, Bob. *Those Wonderful Days. Tales of Racing's Golden Era*. New York: Amerpub Co. (1976), p.88;

Tracy, Len. "Memoirs of the Kentucky Derby." *The Thoroughbred Record*. Issue date unknown; and a Western Union telegram dated October 1, 1945, from Joe Palmer to J.A. Estes, *The Blood-Horse*.

6.   Hollingsworth, Kent. "John E. Madden's Hamburg Place." *The Blood-Horse*. January 16, 1965. p. 151.

7.   Savage, C. J. *Louisville Courier-Journal*. May 12, 1918.

Chapter 4

1.   Frederick, William G. "Scenes in Betting Ring Are Graphically Described by Expert." *Louisville Courier-Journal*. May 12, 1918. Section 5, p. 6.

2.   *The Thoroughbred Record*. March 2, 1918.

3.   Frederick. "Scenes in Betting Ring Are Graphically Described by Expert."; and Pearce, Walter H. "Kilmer Colt Wins Classic at Long Odds." *Louisville Courier-Journal*. May 12, 1918. p. 1.

4.   Savage, C.J. "Exterminator Brought $1,500 as Yearling at Saratoga." *Louisville Courier-Journal*. May 12, 1918, Section 5, p. 2.

5.   Clark, John H. "Dragging Old Bones Out of the Closet." *The Thoroughbred Record*. Date unknown.

6.   Tracy, Len. "Memoirs of the Kentucky Derby." *The Thoroughbred Record*. Date unknown.

7.   Savage. Ibid.

8.   Ibid.

9.   *New York Herald*, September 7, 1919. p. 6.

Chapter 5

1.   "Horse as Factor in War." *The Thoroughbred Record*. February 16, 1918. In *Hoofprints of the Century*. p. 199.

2.   Ibid.

3.   "From Saratoga." *New York Daily Tribune*. August 11, 1865. In Edward Hotaling, *They're Off: Horse Racing at Saratoga*. Syracuse, N.Y.: Syracuse University Press (1995), p. 66.

4.   *The Saratogian*. Saratoga Springs, N.Y. July 27, 1918.

5.   *The Saratogian*. August 22, 1918.

6.   *The Saratogian*. August 27, 1918; and the *New York Herald*. August 27, 1918.

Chapter 7

1.   Hildreth, Samuel C. and Crowell, James R. *The Spell of the Turf*. Philadelphia: J.B. Lippincott Co. (1926), p. 237. Hindoo (1878) won twelve races at or beyond a mile and a half.

2.   *The New York Times*. October 12, 1919.

Chapter 8

1.   *The Sun and New York Herald*. August 1, 1920.

2.   Ross. *Boots and Saddles*. pp 191-192.

Chapter 9

1. Newman, Neil. "Exterminator: His Steadiness Made him America's Favorite." *The Blood-Horse.* November 27, 1948. p. 558.
2. Dunstan, Nelson. "The Derby's Greatest Romance." *Turf and Sport Digest,* May 1936. p. 74.
3. Ibid.
4. Wade, Horace. "One Tough Bag of Bones." *Spur.* November/December 1983. p. 61.

Chapter 10

1. Copyrighted c. 2001 by Daily Racing Form, Inc. and Equibase Company. Reprinted with Permission of the Copyright owner.
2. Newman, Neil. "Great Cup Horses. Number 4: Exterminator." *Morning Telegraph.* March 29, 1935. Copyrighted c. 2001 by Daily Racing Form, Inc. and Equibase Company.
3. Ibid.
4. "Racing in Chicago." *The Thoroughbred Record.* October 7, 1922. p. 170.
5. Copyrighted c. 2001 by Daily Racing Form, Inc. and Equibase Company.
6. Copyrighted c. 2001 by Daily Racing Form, Inc. and Equibase Company.
7. Newman. "I Remember. McDaniel Recalls Mighty Deeds of Gallant Gelding, Exterminator." *Morning Telegraph.* July 16, 1934.

Chapter 11

1. Newman. "I Remember. McDaniel Recalls Mighty Deeds of Gallant Gelding, Exterminator."
2. Welch, Ned. *Who's Who in Thoroughbred Racing.* Volume II. Washington, D.C.: Who's Who in Thoroughbred Racing, Inc. (1947), p. 177.
3. Hirsch, Joe. "100th Anniversary Daily Racing Form: A Special Anniversary Collector's Edition." November 17, 1994. p. 39. Copyrighted 2001 by Daily Racing Form, Inc.

Chapter 12

1. Chowning, Larry S. *Southside Sentinel.* Urbana, Virginia. July 21, 1983. pp. 1-2.
2. Shay, Jack. "Was He the Greatest Racehorse? Maybe He Was Just the Best." *Binghamton Press.* May 7, 1978. p. 8.
3. Chowning. p. 1.
4. Ibid. p. 2.
5. "Kilmer's Steenth Trainer." *The Blood-Horse.* July 25, 1931. p. 105.
6. Priore, Louise M. "Mike Terry and West Side Kids Chief Mourners as Famed 'Old Bones' Passes." *Binghamton Press.* September 26, 1945.

Index

EXTERMINATOR

ACKNOWLEDGMENTS

When I began my research on Exterminator, I knew it wouldn't be easy clearing up some of the stories which over the many decades had become difficult to distinguish between fact and myth. So immediately I went to Phillipians 4:13: "I can do all things through Christ who strengthens me."

The first two places and people I contacted were familiar ones, having helped me before: the Keeneland Library in Lexington, Kentucky, and Dorothy Ours and Tom Gilcoyne at the Museum of Racing and Hall of Fame in Saratoga Springs, New York. Phyllis Rogers and Cathy Schenck, librarians at Keeneland, sent me a multitude of information on the history of racing in Lexington and the old Kentucky Association track.

Dorothy Ours, education assistant, had helped me on *Native Dancer*, and came through with loads of newspaper material from 1919 and 1920, as well as information on Saratoga, yearling sales, and what have you. She introduced me to Jeanne Williams, assistant curator of education and coordinator of public programs, and what a gem! Binghamton, New York, is her hometown. She spent hours taking photos, some appearing in this book; tracking down people and articles, as well as presenting me with a copy of the book, *Saratoga Lost*, by Robert Joki. Jeanne says that Exterminator is her all-time favorite. Tom Gilcoyne, museum volunteer and historian par excellence, was always eager to look up old race charts and other information.

Diane Viert, at *The Blood-Horse*, also tracked down many an old magazine issue for me, and Judy Marchman, assistant editor at Eclipse Press, provided several vital articles. My thanks to Eclipse Press for sending me the Mildred Mastin Pace book on Exterminator, *Kentucky Derby Champion*.

Floyd West, historian for the Broome County Historical Society in Binghamton, had done considerable research on the complex Willis Sharpe Kilmer and shared his papers with me. Maureen Callajhan, in the research archives of the newspaper Kilmer founded,

Binghamton Press, had not heard of Exterminator, but while looking up information for me, became a fan.

Bill Cherry, who participated in Exterminator's 1943 appearance at Belmont Park, was eager to share his experiences; and John McEvoy, his expertise with *Daily Racing Form*. And Paula Welch, who compiled the DRF book, *Champions*. And thanks to trainer John T. Ward, who saddled Monarchos to win the 2001 Kentucky Derby. While fulfilling a busy schedule, he returned my phone call to confirm he was the grandson of John S. Ward, who trained Escoba, one of Exterminator's opponents.

I hope I have left no one out and beseech their forgiveness if I have.

Eva Jolene Boyd

Photo Credits

Cover photo: (The Blood-Horse)

Page 1: Exterminator head shot (Keeneland-Cook); Exterminator (Grayson/Sutcliffe Collection)

Page 2: McGee (Grayson/Sutcliffe Collection); Fair Empress (Grayson/Sutcliffe Collection); Jim Gore (The Blood-Horse)

Page 3: J. Cal Milam and Desha Breckinridge (H.C. Ashby); Milam with Merrick (The Blood-Horse)

Page 4: Willis Sharpe Kilmer (Foster Disinger); Kilmer Building, Kilmer House (both Jeanne M. Williams)

Page 5: Bill Knapp (Keeneland-Cook); Henry McDaniel (The Blood-Horse)

Page 6: Exterminator with Albert Johnson up (C.C. Cook); With Charlie Fairbrother (Keeneland-Cook); With Bill Kelsay (Keeneland-Cook)

Page 7: Exterminator and Sun Briar (Keeneland-Cook); Exterminator in Derby winner's circle (The Blood-Horse)

Page 8: Sun Briar winning the 1919 Champlain (Keeneland-Cook); Exterminator winning the 1920 Luke Blackburn (Keeneland-Cook)

Page 9: Sir Barton winning the 1920 Saratoga Handicap (Keeneland-Cook); Exterminator winning the 1920 Saratoga Cup (Keeneland-Cook)

Page 10: Exterminator winning the 1920 Autumn Gold Cup (Keeneland-Cook); Exterminator winning the Merchants' and Citizens' Handicap (Keeneland-Cook)

Page 11: Mad Hatter (The Blood-Horse); Exterminator and Mad Hatter (Keeneland-Cook)

Page 12: Exterminator and Be Frank (Keeneland-Cook); Exterminator winning the 1922 Brooklyn (Keeneland-Cook); Exterminator winning the 1922 Saratoga Cup (Keeneland-Cook)

Page 13: Court Manor Stud dispersal (The Blood-Horse)

Page 14: Exterminator and Peanuts at Pimlico (Pimlico Photo)

Page 15: Exterminator with Mike Terry (The Blood-Horse); With Mrs. Willis Kilmer and Peanuts (The Blood-Horse)

Page 16: Gravestone (Jeanne M. Williams); Exterminator conformation (Keeneland-Cook)

ABOUT THE
AUTHOR

Eva Jolene Boyd is a sixth-generation Texan. Born in San Antonio in 1937, she has loved horses her entire life. Assault was the first great racehorse she ever saw in person when she went to King Ranch. Boyd's own horses include a half-Thoroughbred and a little Mexican cow pony.

Boyd's love affair with Thoroughbred racing began in 1953 when she saw the telecast of Native Dancer winning the Gotham Stakes.

She eventually combined her love for both horses and writing. She has had articles published in *The Thoroughbred Record*, *Turf and Sport Digest*, *SPUR*, *The Backstretch*, and *The Blood-Horse*.

In addition to *Exterminator*, Boyd also is the author of *Native Dancer: Thoroughbred Legends*, *That Old Overland Stagecoaching*, and *Noble Brutes: Camels on the American Frontier*. She resides in Ingram, Texas.

Forthcoming titles
in the

THOROUGHBRED
Legends®

series:

Carry Back

Secretariat

Available titles:

Man o' War

Dr. Fager

Citation

Go for Wand

Seattle Slew

Forego

Native Dancer

Nashua

Spectacular Bid

John Henry

Personal Ensign

Sunday Silence

Ruffian

Swaps

Affirmed and Alydar

Round Table

War Admiral